Cain v. Abel

University of Nebraska Press
Lincoln

Cain v. Abel

A Jewish Courtroom Drama

RABBI DAN ORNSTEIN

The Jewish Publication Society
Philadelphia

"Cain and Maples: The Villain's Villanelle," by
Dan Ornstein, *Jewish Literary Journal*, http://
jewishliteraryjournal.com/poetry/cain-and-maples/.
"Cain's (Im)Penitent Response to His Punishment," by
Eliezer Finkelman, TheTorah.com. Poems reproduced
from *Points of Departure* by Dan Pagis, translated by
Stephen Mitchell, English translation copyright 1982 by
The Jewish Publication Society, Philadelphia. Used with
permission.

Manufactured in the United States of America. ∞

Library of Congress Cataloging-in-Publication Data
Names: Ornstein, Dan, author.
Title: Cain v. Abel: a Jewish courtroom drama / Rabbi Dan
Ornstein.
Description: Lincoln: University of Nebraska Press, 2020.
Includes bibliographical references.
Identifiers: LCCN 2019039022
ISBN 9780827614673 (paperback)
ISBN 9780827618374 (epub)
ISBN 9780827618381 (mobi)
ISBN 9780827618398 (pdf)
Subjects: LCSH: Cain (Biblical figure)—Drama. | Abel
(Biblical figure)—Drama. | Bible. Genesis IV—Criticism,
interpretation, etc.
Classification: LCC PS3615.R584 C35 2020
DDC 813/.6—dc23
LC record available at https://lccn.loc.gov/2019039022

Set in Merope by Mikala R. Kolander.

In memory of my father-in-law,
Raymond Alexander

———————————————————

In a place where there are no men,
strive to be one.

—*Pirke Avot: Ethics of the Sages* 2:6

Contents

Acknowledgments

I could not have written this book when I was younger. It took me many years to learn from outstanding people how to be a better writer, a better Jew, and ultimately a better human being. To the following people, I owe my deepest gratitude and love.

My wife, Marian Alexander, and our children, Joseph, Shulamit, and Vered Ornstein. Many thanks to my wife for a number of thoughtful insights about Cain and Abel that have informed the writing of this book, as well as for her unflagging technical assistance.

My parents and siblings, Dr. Sheldon, Sheila, and Marc Ornstein, and Rachel Packer, as well as my siblings' families: Shira, Larry, Marni, Alana, Gilah, David, Leah, and Ari.

My in-laws, Raymond (of blessed memory) and Rosalie Alexander, as well as my siblings-in-law and their families: Karen and Patrick DeOssie, Jerry, Michelle, and Jacob Alexander.

My many aunts, uncles, and cousins, who remind me constantly of the blessings (and at times, the blessed challenges) of extended family.

My dear friends in many places, from Albany, New York, to Jerusalem, Israel.

Rabbi Barry Schwartz, director of The Jewish Publication Society, for encouraging me to write this book and giving me the opportunity to publish it.

Joy Weinberg, managing editor of The Jewish Publication Society, for her keen literary eye, her outstanding editing skills, and teaching me how to be a much better writer.

Leif Milliken, Joeth Zucco, Ginny Perrin, and the entire staff of the University of Nebraska Press for their fine work bringing this book to press.

My fellow congregants, friends, and teachers at Congregation Ohav Shalom in Albany, New York. They have always challenged me intellectually and graciously given me the time and space for writing, study, and contemplation.

Rabbi Rena Halpern Kieval, my co-rabbi at Congregation Ohav Shalom, for our many years of friendship, collegiality, and partnership.

The outstanding administrative staff and educators at Congregation Ohav Shalom, whose support and sense of humor make my rabbinic work successful every day.

My student and friend Claire Sigal, of Albany, New York, for her midrashic insights about what Cain and Abel discussed in the field before the murder. (See chapter 9.)

My colleagues, teachers, congregants, and friends who mentored me as I wrote this book: Rabbi Bradley Artson, Victoria Coe, Rabbi Martin Cohen, Rabbi Eliezer Finkelman, Professor Marilyn Francus, Howard Goldberg, Matthew and Sally Greenblatt, David Liebschutz, Dr. Michael Lozman, Professor Timothy Lytton, Seth Marnin, Nancy Pandolfo, Colleen Piccolino, Rabbi Dennis Ross, Barbara Stein, Professor David Stern, Professor Rose Trentinella, Rabbi Burton Visotzky, and David Weingard.

Special thanks to Rabbi Cohen, Rabbi Neil Gillman (of blessed memory), Rabbi Judith Hauptman, Rabbi Ross, Rabbi Joel Roth, Rabbi Visotzky, Professor Lytton, and Professor Stern for teaching me how to write, teach, and think about Rabbinic literature as a vital spiritual enterprise.

My spiritual directors, Sister Katherine Hanley, CSJ, and Sister Christine Partisano, CSJ.

Also, my deepest thanks to the leadership and staff of the following retreat settings that provided quiet space and sanctuary while I was writing *Cain v. Abel*: Ignatian House in Atlanta, Georgia; Priory Retreat Center in Chestertown, New York; Camp Ramah New England in Palmer, Massachusetts; Red Robin Song Guest House in New Lebanon, New York; Casa San Carlos in Delray, Florida; and Linwood Spiritual Center in Rhinebeck, New York.

You are praised, Adonai our God, Ruler of the universe, for giving us life, for sustaining us, and for bringing us to this blessed time.

Introduction

Reintroducing One of the World's Oldest Crime Stories

Bruce Springsteen had a tortured relationship with his father, Douglas, whose mental illness and resentments about his life poisoned their interactions.[1] Having struggled all his life with severe depression, Springsteen wrote his iconic autobiographical song, "Adam Raised a Cain," using biblical imagery "to summon the hard inheritance handed down from father to son."[2]

It's not surprising that Springsteen employed the biblical Cain and Abel story to describe how his father's demons became his own. "Adam Raised a Cain" continues a great legacy of creative interpretations of the Cain and Abel story that address our struggles with rivalry, dysfunction, and violence within our nuclear, extended, and wider human families. William Shakespeare alluded directly to Abel's murder in *Hamlet*, his tragic play about the prince of Denmark who seeks revenge on his uncle for committing adultery with his mother and murdering his father.[3] John Steinbeck devoted his classic novel *East of Eden* to retelling the story in a contemporary context. Thomas Hardy used themes from the story in his great novels *Far from the Madding Crowd* and *The Mayor of Casterbridge*. Elvis Costello's song "Blame It on Cain (Don't Blame It on Me)" comments on criminals' excuses for their behavior. Stephen Dobyns's poem "Long Story" is a chilling and insightful take on Cain's (and all people's) postmortem excuse making. Some of the Western world's most striking paintings and sculptures depict Cain's murder of Abel, among them works by Peter Paul Rubens (1608–9), Titian (1542–44), Jan and Hubert Van Eyck (1425–29), Jacopo Tintoretto (1550–53), William Blake (1826), and Marc Chagall (1960).

This book is my contribution to that interpretive tradition, part of our ongoing attempt to ask and answer the most important questions about violence within the human family.

How *Cain v. Abel* Came to Be

Once, when I was in a criminal courtroom as part of jury duty service, the judge's admonishment to all of us potential jurors made a particularly deep impression on me. Before he began what would turn out to be several hours of tortuously slow jury selection, he said to us, "I know that this process will be very boring, but it is one of the most significant things you will ever do in your lives. If you are selected for this jury, you will have a tremendous responsibility placed upon your shoulders."

At that moment I glanced over at the defendant and realized that no matter how carefully the judge and lawyers selected the twelve jurors, his well-being would lie in that jury's all-too-human hands. The jury's sense of fairness in judging the facts and testimony would be critical to his life. The judge's admonition reminded me of a famous passage in the Mishnah (the compendium of ancient Jewish law and legal argument) that cites the story of Cain and Abel to warn witnesses to capital crimes about the gravity of their testimony.

In the Land of Israel of ancient times, capital cases—those in which the accused could be executed if convicted—encompassed crimes as diverse as murder, idolatry, adultery, even violations of the Sabbath (a ritual prohibition). Jewish law does not provide for what we would recognize as a jury of one's peers, but the Torah does require capital cases to be tried with no fewer than two witnesses (Deut. 7:16).[4] Ancient Jewish communities in the Land of Israel tried capital cases before regional courts with twenty-three sitting judges. If necessary, a capital case could be brought as far as the Great Sanhedrin, the Jewish "supreme" court, where seventy-one judges sat in session in the Holy Temple in Jerusalem (and later, after the Romans' destruction of the Temple in 70 CE, in other locales).

The Mishnah and its later running commentary, the Gemara, record the great caution with which these capital cases proceeded. In principle, a person could be put to death for a crime, but in reality, Jewish law made it very difficult for this to happen. When witnesses in a capital case were interrogated and vetted before a trial, as part of the judges' warning to them about not providing false or inaccurate testimony, they were admonished with these words:

> In civil cases (involving payment) a person can pay money and make restitution. In capital cases, the witness is answerable for the blood of the defendant who is wrongfully condemned to death, as well as that of his offspring.
>
> We learn this from the story of when Cain killed his brother, Abel. There, the Bible tells us that God said to Cain, "Hark, *your brother's blood* cries out to Me from the ground."
>
> The Bible literally writes, "*Your brother's bloods* [in the plural in Hebrew]. This means that Cain not only spilled Abel's blood, but also the blood of his potential descendants who would never be born.[5]

Note how the judges of ancient Jewish times used an extremely literal reading of the Hebrew word for blood to make a compelling moral point. Taking the life of an innocent person destroys not only that person but also his or her potential descendants. The murdered person's blood, as well as that of the progeny who will never be born, cries out from the ground to God, demanding justice.

To the best of my knowledge, this is the only time that the story of Cain and Abel appears in a Jewish *legal* proceeding or record.[6] Jewish law could have used other quotations from the Bible to warn potential witnesses against treating the life of an accused person in a cavalier way. Why was Cain and Abel's story used in a legal teaching about court proceedings?

I suggest that the Mishnah chose the story of Cain and Abel, an extreme case, to make a crucial point about justice. The biblical story relates the horrible consequences of allowing our anger and other passions to drive us to take an *innocent* life. Now, consider the courtroom context in which it is retold. Here, the person who could become the victim of murder is not a crime victim but a potential victim of justice gone awry—that is, the accused who is *under suspicion* of taking an innocent life. In admonishing the witnesses this way, the Mishnah is making an analogy to the ease with which Cain committed the first murder against his own brother. The Mishnah wants us to think likewise about how easy it would be for us, as witnesses or as members of the jury, to kill a person accused of a terrible crime. The defendant standing before us might have committed the crime, but we cannot be sure of that yet, without first hearing and weighing the evidence. Our righteous indignation, vengefulness, biases, or apathy could easily get in the way of our fair and impartial judgment. By treating the accused as if he or she were Cain, without considering the facts and the grave consequences of our potential actions, we would become Cain, and the accused would become Abel.

I thought about this insight as I sat in court watching the process of jury selection. Although this was not a capital case, the jury's decision might irrevocably change the defendant's life. Would we, the jurors (if in fact assigned to this case), safeguard the rights and life of this defendant? Would we, the jurors, simply dismiss this person as guilty, by assuming uncritically or self-righteously that he or she must bear the proverbial "mark of Cain"?[7] If so, what would this say about us, the supposed defenders of all the Abels, the other innocent people of the world? I began to understand that Jewish tradition is challenging us to explore with great care Cain's crime, our capacity for fair judgment, and how we use Cain and Abel's story to tell our own stories.

That story, here restructured as a courtroom drama, grew out of these insights.

We the Jury

Notably, the biblical passage in Genesis 4:1–16—what this book calls the "crime report"—uses crime detective/courtroom imagery. God warns Cain not to behave criminally; Cain commits murder; God proceeds to interrogate and then punish him for it; and Cain throws himself on the mercy of the court, as it were, begging God for clemency in his sentencing.

This work imagines that sentencing taking place in the context of a Jewish courtroom drama. In effect, it is a modern-day version of midrash, the classical creative Jewish interpretation of the Bible. Midrash has long been employed to flesh out "bare-bones" narratives like the Cain and Abel story by imagining the main characters speaking and acting in ways not made explicit in the biblical text. Midrash may also place absent characters in the account as part of developing an instructive or enlightening backstory.

With this midrash I hope to inspire each of us to imagine ourselves as jurors in Cain's murder trial. As jurors, we are expected to weigh evidence and establish the facts as well as the mitigating circumstances to the best of our ability. Putting the world's first sibling on trial for the world's first murder allows us to judge Cain's behavior, but also to judge our own, in and out of the courtroom.

In our case, we will call Cain and a variety of expert witnesses to the witness stand. Though Cain's culpability for the murder has already been established, his crime is not sui generis; it happened in the context of his family's life and history, his relationship with God, God's relationship with creation, and Cain's encounter with the impulse to sin. To understand Cain is not to excuse him, but to deepen our understanding of why we human beings do what we do. Many of the expert witnesses in this trial will be great Rabbis of ancient and medieval times who commented insightfully about the story; others will be modern scholars. Much of the time, the witnesses will not agree.

For the ancient and medieval Rabbis, the Bible contained the deepest eternal wisdom because it came from God. They quoted this wisdom frequently as the basis for their teachings. They were also bold spiritual thinkers who often radically reinterpreted biblical texts in order to teach ideas and values. They felt strongly that God not only permitted but expected them to actively interpret the texts. A close examination of their sometimes audacious explanations through the creative vehicle of witness testimony will hopefully breathe new life into the Cain and Abel story.

To help us make sense of the varying interpretations, each imaginary transcript of in-court testimony will be followed by brief commentaries. Together, these arguments and analyses are designed to help readers, "we, the jury," to ask good questions about Cain's behavior, and its broader implications for us all. Put succinctly, this process should help us to confront three questions about this story: What does it say, what are its possible meanings, and what might it mean for us today?

As you read these transcripts, I hope you will ask your own probing questions about Cain and Abel and do your own contemporary midrash, deriving meanings and teachings that are personally important to you.

Studying Cain and Abel's Bloody Story

Though it is an ancient narrative, the Cain and Abel story sends us the timeless message that jealousy and murderous hatred between people have always been part of the human family's condition. It is a primary source for thoughtful study and courageous conversation about what it means to be human, how we might control our worst impulses, and what responsibilities we bear for one another.

In some ways, our time is no different than the era in which Cain and Abel was written. What has changed is the rapidity with which human hatred can be dispatched to sow destruction anywhere in the world. We have never been as effective as we are now at using our big brains and our most advanced tools to perpetuate so much evil so easily against each other.

As individuals, we might therefore feel we lack the influence to combat human violence and to effect positive change on a global level. However, each of us still plays a critical role in effecting change, through how we behave toward others in our daily lives. The popular contemporary Jewish concept of *tikkun olam*, "repairing the world" through social justice, is founded in part on the mystical idea that each Jewish person helps God to heal the cosmos through mitzvot, Jewish ritual and ethical commandments and practices. Yet *tikkun olam* takes place concurrently with what some teachers of Jewish spirituality call *tikkun atzmi*, "self-repair." According to these teachers, *tikkun atzmi* can be actualized through study, introspection, and cultivating good character and behavior.[8]

I suggest that the story of Cain and Abel appears in the Bible to challenge every generation of readers—Jews and, by extension, all human beings—to work at both kinds of repair.

Though I approach this story through the lens of Judaism and its textual sources (as a religious Jew and a rabbi, these are what I know best), I invite people of all faiths, of no specific faith, and/or of no faith to read and study the story with me. Bring your insights and the wisdom of your own traditions to the discussion. Most of all, bring your most open selves.

Asking Hard Questions

Being fully engaged in this story means asking hard questions about the biblical text.

One central question is why Eve and Adam, the parents of Cain and Abel, are almost entirely absent from it. To fully understand Cain and Abel, and ourselves by extension, I contend that we must explore this strange feature very carefully. We would expect Eve and Adam to play important roles in their sons' lives and fatal encounter, but the two appear only at the outset of the narrative, before the story of the brothers' relationship begins, and at the end, after God has banished Cain for murdering his brother.

In the chapters that follow, we will imaginatively relocate Eve and Adam in this story and look at four different reasons why the Bible might have excluded Eve and Adam from the main parts of the original tale. This exploration will help us to answer another central question: To what extent should our parents' actions (and inactions) define who we are and what we might become?

Three other central questions running though this book are whether God's warning to Cain about not succumbing to Sin was sufficiently clear to Cain before he killed his brother; whether or not Cain was sufficiently morally free when he murdered Abel to be fully culpable for his crime; and what might the presence of Sin, the character notorious for inciting Cain's murderousness, be teaching us about our own worst (and best) impulses?

This exploration will help us to understand more deeply why God punished Cain in the ways described by the biblical story. It will also facilitate further discussion about how we balance culpability against mitigating factors (what Judaism calls "justice versus mercy") in determining our relationship with people who do wrong.

The Ultimate Hard Question?

There is a great Jewish legend about two warring schools of angels who argued with God.

The story grows out of the ancient Rabbis' deep puzzlement concerning Genesis 1:27, "*Na'aseh Adam b'tzalmeinu* [Let *us* create humans in *our* image]." The Rabbis wanted to know to whom God was referring when God used the terms "us" and "our." While God might have been employing the majestic plural, or "Royal We," to refer to God's Self, the Rabbis offered a much more intriguing explanation: God was taking advice from the angels, the celestial beings of ancient Jewish legend who were a sort of divine entourage. Whereas in English God's words constitute a declarative statement, "Let us create humans in our image," in the original Hebrew the words could also be read as a question: "I want to know what you angels think. *Should* we create human beings in our image?"

One Rabbinic Sage explained just how controversial the creation of human beings was and continues to be:

> Rabbi Simon said: When God was about to create the first human, the ministering angels formed themselves into factions and groups.
>
> Some of them said: "Let him be created." Some of them said: "Let him not be created."
>
> Lovingkindness said, "Let him be created because he will perform acts of lovingkindness."
>
> Truth said, "Let him not be created because he will be all falsehood."
>
> Justice said, "Let him be created because he will do deeds of justice."
>
> Peace said, "Let him not be created because he will be all conflict."
>
> What did God do? God took Truth and cast him to the ground.
>
> The ministering angels said to God: "Master of the Universe: Why do You humiliate Your chief of staff? Lift Truth up from the earth!" . . .
>
> R. Huna the elder of the city of Tzippori said: "While the ministering angels were debating each other, and conferring with each other, God made the human and said to them: 'What are you debating? The human being has already been created!'"[9]

My teacher Rabbi Burton Visotzky explains that these ministering angels are symbols of four conflicting values that reside "within" God and the world. The storyteller turns them into "arguing" angels as a concrete demonstration of the agonizing complexity and moral ambiguity of the human condition. Almost anticipating Cain and

Abel's story, the four angelic counselors face off in stark opposition: "God, create these humans and you will have Your hands full of their violence and lies." Or, "God, these humans will have the potential to act with justice and compassion. It is worth it to create them."

Rabbi Visotzky points out that this story, like the many Rabbinic stories comparing God to a king, takes a veiled poke at the leaders of the Roman Empire, whose reputations were familiar to the Jews of Greco-Roman Palestine, where this legend originated. Emperors and governors would officially take counsel with their appointed advisors, but it was the worst-kept secret of the empire that these advisors' roles were a sham. Roman leaders, emperors especially, saw themselves as gods. They worked alone and never took advice from anyone. The Sages' point was to show how the real Emperor, God, truly works alone. Notwithstanding all of the angels' vociferous advice for and against creating people, God, the one true Ruler, had already planned to create us.[10]

In setting this book's courtroom scenes, I have imagined the aforementioned angels as our legal teams. The main two litigators are Truth, the prosecuting attorney, who will condemn humanity as hopelessly dishonest and violent; and Lovingkindness, Cain's defense attorney, who will defend humanity's potential to be just and kind. In the courtroom, Truth and Lovingkindness will exercise all of their ingenuity to convince the jury to accept their diametrically opposed portrayals of Cain's character and motivations for murder. Truth will insist that Cain deserves the severest punishment; Lovingkindness will demand that Cain deserves the greatest clemency. Notably, both Truth and Lovingkindness will draw their arguments not only from the evidence proffered in the crime report but also from their antithetically opposed approaches to the worthiness of human life. Cain's trial is a test case for their fierce, ongoing debate before God, encapsulated in perhaps the hardest question of all: Given how morally unpredictable and unreliable human beings are, should God have created people in the first place?

Notes for Reading This Book

The great American rabbi and thinker Mordecai Kaplan once said that "the foremost problem of Jewish religion is how to get Jews to take the Bible seriously without taking it literally."[11] He wanted readers of the Bible to stop dwelling on whether or not the stories were historically or scientifically true and to focus instead on the stories' enduring truths.

For example, we will probably never know if an actual family comprising Eve and Adam and their sons, Cain and Abel, lived at one time. It seems more likely than not that such a family never existed. In all probability this biblical family serves as a mythic prototype of how human families might and do behave.

As another example, although Jewish interpreters have devised some inventive explanations,[12] we will likely never figure out how Cain could have had offspring. According to the Bible, he, his brother, and their parents were the only people in the world. Living before the establishment of divine law and rules, did they have incestuous relations with Eve or with their twin sisters, as imagined by Rabbinic literature? In my view, struggling with these kinds of questions about this story is not important. It helps to consider that Cain and Abel (and other biblical accounts) are true because their insights about being human are profoundly true and timelessly relevant. This story might be fiction. Its wisdom isn't.

Note that in the book I use the terms "Torah" (lit., "instruction") and "Bible" somewhat interchangeably. Technically, though, Torah refers to the Five Books of Moses: Genesis, Exodus, Leviticus, Numbers, and Deuteronomy. These first five books in the Bible cover Israelite history and law from the creation of the world until Moses' death and the people's entrance into the Promised Land. For Jews the Bible refers to the corpus of twenty-four biblical books divided into three sections: the Torah, the books of the Prophets (such as Isaiah and Jeremiah), and the collected writings (such as Psalms and

Proverbs). Collectively, this corpus is known by the Hebrew acronym TANAKH: **T**orah, **N**evi'im (Prophets), **K**ethuvim (Writings).

A word about chronological order, or what seems to be disorder. The Rabbis of ancient talmudic literature established the principle that the Torah does not follow a strict chronological order.[13] They believed that the time sequence of biblical narratives, both legal and nonlegal, is often flexible. Somewhat comparable in style to a magical realist novel, past, present, and future scenes are often placed next to each other with no regard for which scene is earlier or later. For our purposes, this allows for Torah passages to be understood in new ways, and thus reveal new and refreshing meanings in stories. Later Rabbinic literature can be said to follow this same principle, by allowing Sages from different time periods to discuss and argue with each other on each page of the Talmud and in parallel midrashic collections. Similarly, the imaginary courtroom scenes in this volume allow teachers of the tradition from different eras to speak to one another, and to us.

Finally, a brief word about God, or more specifically, the complex image of God that I present in this book. We often imagine God as the unchanging and "unmoved Mover" Who is all-powerful, all-knowing, all-good, and all-present throughout the universe; at least we pay lip service to these beliefs. These are classical Jewish God concepts whose roots we can detect in the earliest strata of Jewish history and thought. However, they mostly reflect the theologies of Jewish thinkers of the Middle Ages who attempted to apply rigorous philosophical frameworks to understanding God. The God of the Bible and the later Rabbis is far less consistent and easy to categorize. In *Cain v. Abel*, I portray God as full of emotion, mystery, passion, and even imperfection in dealing with human beings. This is because the Bible and its Rabbinic interpreters often portray God in these ways; this is especially so when God is dealing with a humanity that is radically free to make its own messy, unpredictable moral and behavioral decisions. You might be uncomfortable at first with this "messier" description of God. However, consider that, in many respects, this image of God is far more dynamic and, in my opinion, much more interesting. God, the Creator of Cain, Abel, their parents, and all people, can and does enter relationships with us. As we know, relationships can be quite dynamic and messy.

Unless otherwise noted, all Bible text translations are from the *Jewish Publication Society Hebrew-English TANAKH* (1999). Unless otherwise noted, all other text translations are by this author.

Getting the Most from This Book

To use this book productively, I recommend you read it with the understanding that we are entering the world of biblical and Jewish legendary myth. As you read, ask yourself: *What are the story and its interpreters trying to say?*

After you have absorbed these readings, good conversation will enrich your insights and experiences. Here are a few ways to foster that conversation:

Do a staged or informal reading of one or more of the courtroom transcripts. Assign each character to a different reader and have all others in your group serve as the jury. Afterward, discuss if and/or how the scene(s) informed your perspective on the story. For specific scene ideas and questions, consult the activity section of this book's Discussion and Activity Guide.

Select and discuss some of the ethical discussion questions in the Discussion and Activity Guide. These questions are open-ended to stimulate personal engagement, and organized by chapter to facilitate classroom use.

Discuss how you personally relate to this material by selecting a relevant scenario from the activity section of the Discussion and Activity Guide. For example, lawmakers or police officers might consider the guide question: "Are any established laws truly effective in preventing Cain from murdering Abel in every generation?" Psychologists might consider: "Might the story have had a happier ending had Cain received emotional support from his family, his society, and/or his God?" Clergy might weigh: "Why would God create Sin with the power to seduce people into evil behavior, then warn humans to control our sinful impulses?" Feminist thinkers might deliberate: "Would the Cain and Abel story have turned out differently had the two siblings been sisters?" The guide offers many other entry points as well.

Design your own questions, exercises, and activities that address salient points in the story. This includes points I may have missed altogether.

Make a list of themes or ideas embedded in the courtroom drama, then select a few of your and/or others' choice ideas for exploration.

Select a few texts from Jewish tradition highlighted in the book for discussion. Read them multiple times, with and without my commentaries on them. Draw up a series of questions about one of these texts that help you to think about the point or points it might be making. Be careful not to fall into what I call "the humility trap": assuming that, if you lack formal knowledge of this text or of Jewish religious texts in general, you have nothing to say about it. Jewish tradition is emphatic that teachers learn the most from students, and I can personally attest to the fresh, often radical insights I've learned from my students who had no prior background, as we learned these texts together.

When you are ready, move on to perhaps the most important question: What does the Cain and Abel story mean to me and to us/humankind?

Ultimately, I hope that Cain and Abel's story will become a mirror for you to reflect on your own story and the stories of all those people with whom you work and live, whom you love, like, or hate. Further, I hope you will bring with you not only your own identities and loyalties but also the recognition that you and I and indeed all of us are members of one human community seeking to make a better world.

Cain v. Abel

1

Reading Cain and Abel

You might assume that the Bible has nothing to say to you, perhaps because its language or ideas seem foreign and intimidating, it is "too religious," or it lacks the sophistication of other literary works. These assumptions are unfortunate when we consider how deeply indebted to the Bible Western literature is. The author Marilynne Robinson writes that from the earliest "primordial quarrel" of Cain and Abel to the stories of Jesus' encounters with strangers, biblical literature has influenced the greatest writers to look more deeply at human civilization in all its complexity. Bible stories are more than metaphoric or literary window dressing; they are the underpinnings of a profound literary and moral tradition that seeks out meaning through reading and interpreting those stories.[1] The stories might confuse or disturb us, but if we give them a chance, they have a lot to convey.

The core story of Cain's conflict with Abel occupies a mere sixteen verses of the biblical book of Genesis.[2] As you read it ("The Crime Report," below), imagine that you are reading the written record of what happened at the crime scene where one brother murdered the other.

One note about the biblical background to the story. When we meet Cain and Abel, their parents, Eve and Adam, have been banished from the Garden of Eden, that paradise in which all living things existed in perfect harmony until the two ate from the forbidden

Tree of Knowledge of Good and Evil. God banishes Eve and Adam because by having acquired potentially endless knowledge, they have become too much like God. ("Knowledge of good and evil" is likely the Bible's way of saying, "knowledge of everything from A to Z.") Furthermore, if, having already disobeyed one divine order, Eve and Adam go on to eat from the forbidden Tree of Eternal Life, their immortality will make them direct competitors with God for divinity.

Outside Eden, in the real world of adult responsibility, knowledge, and imperfection, Eve and Adam give birth to these two boys, Cain and Abel. We find out more about Eve, Adam, and the Garden later in this book. Right now, the brothers are our focus.

The "Crime Report": Genesis 4:1–16

Now the man knew his wife Eve, and she conceived and bore Cain, saying, "I have gained a male child with the help of the Lord." She then bore his brother Abel. Abel became a keeper of sheep, and Cain became a tiller of the soil.

In the course of time, Cain brought an offering to God from the fruit of the soil; and Abel, for his part, brought the choicest of the firstlings of his flock. God paid heed to Abel and his offering, but to Cain and his offering God paid no heed. Cain was much distressed and his face fell. And God said to Cain,

> "Why are you distressed,
> And why is your face fallen?
> Surely, if you do right
> There is uplift.
> But if you do not do right
> Sin couches at the door;[3]
> Its urge is toward you,
> Yet you can be its master."

Cain said to his brother Abel . . . and when they were in the field, Cain set upon his brother Abel and killed him. God said to

Cain, "Where is your brother Abel?" And he said, "I do not know. Am I my brother's keeper?" Then God said, "What have you done? Hark, your brother's blood cries out to me from the ground! Therefore, you shall be more cursed than the ground, which opened its mouth to receive your brother's blood from your hand. If you till the soil, it shall no longer yield its strength to you. You shall become a ceaseless wanderer on earth."

Cain said to God, "My punishment is too great to bear! Since You have banished me this day from the soil, and I must avoid Your presence and become a restless wanderer on earth—anyone who meets me may kill me!" God said to him, "I promise, if anyone kills Cain, sevenfold vengeance shall be taken on him." And God put a mark on Cain, lest anyone who met him should kill him. Cain left the presence of God and settled in the land of Nod, east of Eden.[4]

Some religious readers assume that the Bible's divine origin severely limits the right of human beings to actively interpret stories such as Cain and Abel. They subject the biblical text to rigidly literalist interpretations, or they presume that it *must* mean what earlier teachers of their tradition have said it means, with no room for more expansive readings. Some secular readers can be no less rigid and simplistic. They often dismiss the profundity of biblical stories like this one because they have been taught to think that the Bible must either be literally true or pure nonsense. Given the polarized choice between these two perspectives, they choose to view it all as nonsense. Neither approach is an accurate reflection of Judaism.

An authentic Jewish approach employs close reading and midrash to better understand the words and ideas of a text, and to recognize in the text myriad layers of hidden meaning waiting to be made manifest. The word "midrash" has its source in the Hebrew verb root *d-r-sh*, to actively inquire or demand an inquiry. Rather than take the meaning of the text on faith or assume we know what it means, we are permitted, even obligated, to inquire and investigate what the text might be teaching us. We begin that process with *great questions* about the text.

At the end of this book you will find a Discussion and Activity Guide containing questions to stimulate individual and group discussion about Cain and Abel. For now, we should consider a few excellent questions raised by one of our expert witnesses: the nineteenth-century Torah scholar and educator Rabbi Meir Leibush Weisser (Russia and Romania, 1809–1879), also known by his acronym, Malbim. A unique feature of his Bible commentary is that he often prefaced his interpretations with questions about discrete segments of the passage he was interpreting. In a sense, Rabbi Weisser's questions are his own study guide. Here are his questions about Cain and Abel from his commentary on Genesis 4:

After this story, Cain's father, Adam, is referred to in the Hebrew text without the definite article preceding his name: (*Adam*, "a man" and not *Ha-Adam*, "the man.") Why this change?

Why did God pay heed to Abel's offering but not to Cain's offering?

Why was God referred to only as "God" (Elohim) in Genesis, chapter one, as "the Lord, God" (Adonai Elohim) in chapter two, and here in the story of Cain and Abel as "the Lord" (Adonai) only?

Why did the Torah write (almost as an afterthought) that Eve then bore Abel?

Why did the Torah not explain the source of Abel's name?

Why did the Torah use such strange language to describe Abel bringing an offering: "And Abel, for his part, (literally, 'even he') brought an offering"?

Why did God question Cain about his being distressed? Was it not reasonable for him to feel that way, given that his offering was rejected?

"Surely, if you do right / There is uplift. / But if you do not do right / Sin couches at the door." This phrase is extremely difficult to understand.

The Torah wrote, "Cain said to Abel . . . ," but it never told us what Cain said to him.

What was Cain's reason for murdering Abel? What did Abel do to him?

When asked about Abel's whereabouts, Cain claimed to God, "I do not know." How could he have lied to God?

God told Cain, "You shall be more cursed than the ground." Why did God curse the ground? Does the ground possess free will, that she should be subjected to reward and punishment like a human being?

Why did Cain protest to God that "Anyone who finds me may kill me"? Wouldn't this be fair punishment for spilling your brother's blood?

Why did God place a mark on Cain as a form of punishment? Is it not the case that a murderer can only receive atonement for his crime through his own blood being spilled?

Why did the Torah tell us that Cain built a city and named it after his son?[5] [This story comes after verse 16.]

Note the breadth of Rabbi Weisser's inquiries. In exploring Cain and Abel's story, he did not limit himself to spiritual concerns, but also raised concerns about difficult grammar and syntax, gaps in the dialogue, Abel's identity, Cain's psychology, and moral freedom.

One of his most intriguing questions, his very first on the chapter, is about the different names and combinations of names for God found in the early Genesis stories. Rabbi Weisser was hardly alone in asking this. Rather, he was following ancient Jewish traditions about the various meanings of God's names in different contexts and scenes. Interestingly, within three years of Rabbi Weisser's death, the most prominent of early modern Christian Bible critics, Julius Wellhausen, would respond to remarkably similar questions. Drawing upon critical Bible scholarship from at least as far back as the philosopher Baruch Spinoza (Netherlands, 1632–1677), Wellhausen viewed the different names for God as partial evidence that the Bible's stories were written separately and then edited together in one composite story many centuries after Moses.[6] To scholars such as Wellhausen, the Torah was a cultural document written by different Israelites over many centuries, which moderns should study as literature and scan for its poetic and spiritual value.[7]

These ideas would have been utter heresy to Rabbi Weisser. For him, the Torah was solely God's unified word, dictated to Moses during the Israelites' forty-year trek to Canaan, to be heeded and obeyed.

Thus it was that the rabbi, a staunch Jewish traditionalist, and the critics, Christian and secularist radicals for their time, shared a passionate commitment to that most Jewish of intellectual endeavors: asking the best questions, out of a commitment to critical inquiry and active engagement with Scripture.

Like that terrible place where Cain murdered his brother, Cain and Abel's story—the words of our crime report—is a wide-open field, full of new and some potentially agonizing revelations. We the jury are called to walk through that killing field, where terrible things about the human past, present, and future will confront us. We too must listen carefully to the voices of our tortured first family, collect evidence from the crime scene, and ask the best questions: of the witnesses, the experts, the accused, and even God.

Our doing so is not a mere intellectual exercise. It is a supreme act of human compassion and courage to seek to balance our quest for justice with our desire to execute that justice mercifully. The judge and the legal teams are calling the jury to attention, for we are about to receive an admonition about justice and mercy before we decide Cain's fate.

2

Balancing Justice and Mercy

An Admonition to the Jury

As an idealistic teenager who thought a lot about injustice, racism, and poverty, I was very impressed by Humphrey Bogart's courtroom performance in the rather melodramatic 1949 noir film *Knock on Any Door*. Bogart plays Andrew Morton, a defense lawyer who takes on the case of Nick Romano (John Derek's breakout role), a young, impoverished thug from the slums accused of murdering a police officer. Remorseful for poorly defending Nick's father years earlier and convinced that society shares Nick's blame for his life of crime, Morton pleads with the jury for clemency in his closing arguments: "Until we do away with the type of neighborhood that produced this boy, ten will spring up to take his place, a hundred, a thousand. Until we wipe out the slums and rebuild them, knock on any door and you may find Nick Romano."[1]

Bogart's call to conscience and compassion on behalf of disenfranchised youth inspired me. I knew many such young people from my inner-city public high school. Implicating society in the crimes that poor and disadvantaged people committed seemed unassailably noble and just to me at age fifteen. At seventeen, though, after I was mugged and then intimidated by one such assailant throughout my senior year, it became much harder for me to be generous in my defense of disenfranchised people who behaved criminally. I carried around a lot of lingering resentment as well as anxiety and fear. I began to see *Knock on Any Door* as just a movie — and in the opinion of at least one critic, a bad movie — not the nuanced and compelling treatment of society's injustices I wanted it to be.[2] I learned what victims of crimes come to understand the hard way: A crime is a brazen, traumatizing act of cruelty and an abuse of power, no matter who commits it or the circumstances of that person's life that led that person to become a criminal. It took me time and maturity to recognize that justice against criminals for their crimes must constantly be balanced against mercy for the sometimes terrible circumstances that contributed to their actions.

Justice and Mercy

The ancient Jewish Sages understood how difficult the interplay between the qualities of justice and mercy could be. They viewed this balancing act not merely as a psychological and moral challenge for people but as a challenge for God in creating and maintaining the world: one with particularly vexing implications for humanity. Earlier, we looked at how one rabbi of ancient times explained God's almost absurd "leap of faith and love" in creating humanity, knowing that people are just as likely to do evil as to do good. In the following story, other Rabbinic Sages portray God as contemplating the creation of flawed humanity even before broaching the subject with the angels (as seen in the aforementioned story). These Rabbis employ the midrashic technique of the *mashal*, interpreting a biblical verse and/or teaching an abstract idea through a suggestive, often purposefully ambiguous parable:

> There was a king who owned some delicate cups.
>
> He said to himself, "If I put hot water into these cups, they will explode. If I put cold water into them they will contract and crack."
>
> The king mixed hot and cold water in the cups so they would not explode or crack, and they did not break.

Similarly, God reasoned, "If I create the world with the quality of mercy only, it will explode from being overrun by unchecked human evil, for I would never punish people. If I create the world with the quality of justice only, it will contract and crack under the pressure of relentless punishment, for I would never forgive people.

Therefore, I will create the world with an even balance of justice and mercy. *Hal'vai*; I should be so lucky that this will allow the world to survive."[3]

The comparison suggested by this *mashal* is incongruous and ambiguous, and the different pieces fit together less than perfectly. God, the Creator of the world, is represented in the story by a king, but even the greatest of human kings could never compare with God. Therefore, why make such a comparison? The world "under construction" is ostensibly represented by the delicate cups: "Something" is going to be poured into them, but in a way that should not destroy them. So, too, human beings require a hospitable moral and spiritual climate, one in which God is neither excessively punishing nor excessively merciful concerning human conduct. God's unchecked mercy and unchecked justice are symbolized by the hot and cold water, respectively. However, both the hot and the cold water are entities separate from the king, whereas mercy and justice are character qualities of God's functioning in the world, even though they are externalized for the purposes of telling this story. Further, even if we accept that God and a human king could be adequately compared for teaching purposes, the king and God *seem to be doing nothing in common*. The king appears to be idly experimenting with water temperatures to figure out how to preserve something he did not create, a behavior we would not even expect of a king. God is grappling with how to apply two powerful, conflicting divine characteristics to sinful human beings, whose lives hang in the balance of divine power. The king successfully pours the lukewarm water into the cups without breaking them. In contrast, most surprisingly, after deciding to create the world and humanity with equal measures of mercy and justice, God sighs, *hal'vai,* "if only," or "I should be so lucky," a possible expression of anxiety about the future of the people and the world that God is about to create. Why would the perfect Creator reflect on creation in this way? Is there a deeper meaning connecting the two parts of this parable? What is it teaching us about justice and mercy, both divine and human?[4]

This parable is known as a "praise *mashal.*" As apologetic praise, it simply celebrates God's power and wisdom in creating the world with fine-tuned balance between justice and mercy so that life can survive.[5] Yet, I want to suggest my own additional, creative reading of the *mashal*'s meaning. The king is indeed experimenting with his fragile cups, but not like some child doing a fun science experiment while indoors on a snowy day. I suggest that the king, whom the Sages likely modeled on the local Roman governors and artisans familiar to them, was testing the strength of glassware.[6] The Sages telling these stories gave their characters considerable descriptive and role flexibility; thus, it is possible that this story is about a king who is also a master glass artisan. The story tells us that the cups are delicate, hinting that they are exquisitely crafted, yet fragile. The king values his work greatly, and simultaneously is too insecure about the cups' strength to take the risk of testing their resilience under the most extreme temperatures. He is assured of the cups' strength solely when he "plays it safe," by putting only lukewarm liquid into them.[7]

All the parts of this story dare us to make bold comparisons and contrasts with God, the Ruler of the universe who is also its Artisan. The critical Hebrew word linking both parts of this *mashal* is *dakim,*[8] the plural adjective for "delicate." Like the glass cups, God's creations are beautiful but delicate to the point of fragility: Likewise, we humans have tremendous potential to do great good but to do great evil as well, which is what gives us our own quality of fragility.

Here is where the simple analogy ends. Unlike the physical temperatures of the hot and cold water being manipulated by the king, God is forever dangerously "running hot and cold" about us. At times God loves us so much that God wants to extend endless mercy to us, even though we run the risk of exploding from unchecked wrongdoing. At other times, God is so enraged by our atrocious behavior that God wants to shut us down with strict justice, to the point where we implode and crack under the pressure of severe punishment. The king's lukewarm solution to his uncertainty about his cups ensures they will last long, but that they will also have little or no functional utility. Not so for God, who has to uphold and balance the two qualities of mercifulness and strictness, for without this delicate balance human beings cannot function fully in the world. An imbalance in favor of either one would mean certain destruction for human existence, so God decides to create us using both characteristics. Unlike the king, God cannot rest easy that this balance will succeed in the future. "Hal'vai," God sighs. "The world and I should be so lucky that the balance holds so that neither of us plunges into chaos."

Our emotional and moral complexities appear to reflect God's inner conflicts as exemplified by this *mashal* story. How could things be otherwise? If humans are created in God's image and likeness, then our struggles to balance justice and mercy, in and out of the courtroom, are, to the best of our knowledge, a human version of God's struggles. Since the moment when Cain spurned mercy for his brother in favor of his anger, which led to humanity's first murder, we too have been trying to achieve that tenuous balance—in our own actions, and when we judge others.

Sitting in the courtroom as the jury, each of us will be admonished by the Defense and the Prosecution to judge with fairness and balance. The Torah's crime report indicates that God warned Cain to control his passions, yet Cain did not do so. Can we understand Cain—his background and emotional struggles—and even view him with compassion and empathy, while still holding him fully guilty and responsible for brutally murdering his brother? Should our more nuanced view of Cain, especially when he confesses his guilt to God, affect how we view his punishment? Should God not be called to account for having created the impulses lurking at the door of Cain's heart—his rage, pride, self-pity, and self-righteousness that seduced him into murder? We the jury might have to question God, "Why did You imbue Cain (and us by extension) with these impulses, only to punish him for using them? Could You have developed greater empathy or equanimity in Cain rather than resentment or anger?" Should we even care about Cain? Shouldn't our compassion for Abel, the victim, take total precedence over any consideration for his brother, the criminal?

As noted, the Mishnah requires that we be exceedingly careful to judge an accused criminal with the utmost fairness. We are to discern every fact in the case before condemning the accused. Our *mashal* story reminds us — and God, as it were — that we must do this by careful calibration of a standard of justice balanced with mercy. This responsibility we have been given is quite onerous, but it is the only way we can bring the fullness of human experience and wisdom to bear on how we deal with each other, in and out of court. *Hal'vai*: We should be so lucky to do this well.

3

Introducing Our Expert Witnesses

Helping us to weigh justice with mercy as we analyze the facts of the case are the Defense and the Prosecution's "expert witnesses": the great teachers of Jewish tradition (some of whose stories we have already encountered).[1] They will help us to examine—and, at times, cross-examine—the six actors who are witnesses to Cain's life and crime: Cain, Sin, Eve, Adam, Abel, and God. Our experts span about two thousand years of Jewish intellectual and religious history, as well as at least three continents. Yet they are united in their attempts to better understand this story of the world's first murder.

The Talmudic Masters

We will hear mostly from teachers who hail from two different Jewish worlds: the early Rabbinic Sages of talmudic literature and the Bible scholars of the Middle Ages.

According to Jewish tradition, midrash has precedents going back to the founding of the Great Assembly, the Jewish governing council of the Land of Israel created by Ezra the scribe in the fourth century BCE. Some midrashic interpretations of the Cain and Abel story "stretch" the meaning of a biblical word or verse beyond what it logically appears to say. Yet the early Rabbis who created and taught them did so in the conviction that the Bible contains the words of the Infinite One, God, and as such the words possess innumerable layers of wisdom and understanding waiting to be mined by us. All of these disparate interpretations are part of the ongoing Jewish conversation about the meaning of Judaism and its sacred texts.

MIDRASHIC WORKS

The early Rabbis' interpretations and insights can be found in two kinds of books: midrashic anthologies and the Talmud (literally, "that which is learned"). Midrashic anthologies are collections of ancient Rabbis' sermons and stories on the Bible in which a biblical verse usually served as the point of departure. The Rabbis taught these sermons and stories in their synagogues during the Sabbath and the Jewish holidays, and in the early Middle Ages they became anthologized as extended commentary on select verses. While the works are often referred to as "the Midrash," this generally means a particular anthology of midrashic insights, for instance, Genesis Rabbah, "the great midrashic book" about Genesis.

As an example of how midrashic teaching works, let's consider the last verse of our story, "Cain left the presence of the Lord and settled in the land of Nod, east of Eden" (Gen. 4:16). The verse implies that Cain, not God, made the ultimate decision to leave Eden, rather than be banished at God's command.[2] It further implies that he could leave God's presence, even though God is everywhere. These apparent problems in the text stimulated (at least) three Sages' responses: "From where did Cain leave? [That is, what could 'Cain left God's presence' possibly mean?]" One said: "He threw ['left'] God's admonitions about his behavior behind him, in an effort to deceive God." A second explained: "He tried to 'leave' God with the false impression that he was penitent." A third avowed: "He left God's presence a happy man, because he sincerely repented and God forgave him."[3]

None of these responses is necessarily the "correct" one. All three attempt to address the ambiguity in this verse in rather fanciful, creative ways that have no provable basis in the Torah's words. In this midrashic teaching, textual accuracy is less relevant than moral instruction. These responses employ the text almost as a pretext for teaching insights about repentance. Each rabbi's interpretation explores the vastly different ways that Cain—and, by extension, all human beings—deal with guilt and punishment. Do we brush off criticism and judgment, instead of learning from our wrongdoing? Do we try to "play" people by feigning contrition for our behavior? Do we have the capacity to repent? And if yes, we do repent, are we able to reclaim genuine joy as the crushing weight of guilt is lifted from us?

Which, if any, of these insights tells the truth about human behavior? Perhaps all of them? This type of interpretive exercise perfectly exemplifies the Rabbinic teaching that the Torah possesses seventy "faces"—that is, numerous dimensions. Torah is the meeting point between divine wisdom and human discovery.

THE TALMUD

Talmudic literature is a vast, elegantly edited record of more than seven centuries' worth of many of these same Rabbis' legal arguments and midrashic stories. It comprises the Mishnah (the Oral Law, a small sample of which we studied above) and the Gemara (arguments and discussions about the Mishnah and Jewish law) as well as stories, maxims, and wisdom teachings. Threaded throughout the Talmud are the same kinds of interpretations and teachings found in the midrashic anthologies. (In fact, both genres often contain parallel versions of the same stories and teachings.)

The talmudic Sages lived in the Jewish communities of Babylonia (present-day Iraq) and the Land of Israel, mostly from the first century BCE through the fifth century CE.[4] Yet examine a page of Talmud and you will discover all of them crossing the boundaries of time and space to take part in a great Jewish dialogue about religious practice, ethics, and theology.

Talmudic arguments utilize highly developed methods of logic and legal reasoning to address significant questions about ritual and ethical behavior as well as the meaning of life. While the Rabbis were not philosophers in any formal sense, they thought about the significance of being human with passion, rigor, and deep insight. They largely engaged in this process through discussions about prooftexts, verses taken from throughout the Bible, to demonstrate the authoritative truth of an idea or legal point.

Consider what appears to be a contradiction between these two verses from our story. What really happens to Cain?

> Cain said to the Lord, "Since You have banished me . . . I must become a restless wanderer on earth!" (Gen. 4:13)

> Cain left the presence of the Lord and settled in the land of Nod, east of Eden. (Gen. 4:16)

In Genesis 4:13, Cain is crying out desperately because God has punished him by casting him into exile as a wanderer. Then how can it be that three verses later, the Torah tells us that Cain has settled in a place called Nod? (Gen. 4:17). From a Rabbinic perspective, God's words are ultimate truth; they cannot contradict each other. In fact, much of midrashic and talmudic literature attempts to resolve contradictory Bible verses and Rabbinic teachings. Could the apparent inconsistency be teaching us something more profound instead, or at least challenging us to ask weighty questions about Cain and Abel as models for human life?

One of the talmudic Sages, the Babylonian rabbi Rav Yehudah, responds to these concerns with an interesting teaching: "Exile atones for half of a person's guilt for wrongdoing. How do we know this? The Torah tells us that, at first, Cain was bitter about being forced to wander, as punishment for his crime. The Torah then tells us that once he atoned for at least part of his sin, he was permitted by God to stop wandering and to settle in Nod."[5]

Rav Yehudah "resolves" the seeming contradiction between our two verses by assigning them to two different stages of Cain's rehabilitation: the penalty phase and after some time served perhaps with some accompanying contrition. At the same time, he tantalizes us, his students, with the provocative idea that the experience of exile can release a person from some measure of his guilt for a committed crime. Such teachings can easily stimulate hours of intense discussion about the human condition that extend well beyond resolving specific textual problems.

Beyond teaching moral lessons, the Rabbis of the Talmud freely interpreted the Bible's verses, phrases, words, and even individual letters (often using explicit interpretive rules) out of the belief that the text holds multiple teachings from God. They held that every text also has a simple meaning based on its immediate context and plain sense—what we call in Hebrew *peshat* ("simple, contextual sense or meaning")—and developed the principle that a biblical passage never loses its simple contextual meaning.[6] Nonetheless, they were committed to delving as deeply into the meanings of God's words as possible, often by taking those words well out of context and engaging in what midrashic scholar Gary Porton refers to as "holy play."[7] This free-form interpretation became known as *derash*, a word related to midrash that means "midrashic or creative meaning."

The Medieval Bible Scholars

The second group of commentators we will call as expert witnesses were faithful inheritors of the interpretive traditions and laws found in the midrashic anthologies and the Talmud. Yet these commentators, known as *parshanim* (those who explain Torah passages), developed a different kind of interpretive scholarship on biblical texts. Rather than rely exclusively on what the Rabbis of the Talmud said about the Torah's meaning, these rabbis sought to determine the *peshat* of its words using the best tools of language scholarship available to them in medieval France, Spain, Israel, or North Africa, where they resided. When an interpretation of the earlier talmudic Rabbis most adequately explained a difficult biblical word or phrase, they noted it. If they could find a better, more logical, or simpler interpretation, even one that opposed the earlier ones, they would note that explanation.[8]

For instance, the Spanish Bible scholar Nachmanides (Spain and Israel, 1194–1270) offers an extremely simple, nonsermonic, and different explanation for "Cain left the presence of the Lord" than the aforementioned more imaginative readings of the earlier Sages. "The plain sense of the verse is that Cain never stood before God anymore, as he meant when he said, 'And I must avoid (lit. be hidden from) Your face.'"[9]

Here, Nachmanides is less concerned with using the verse to teach a lesson and more concerned with explaining the *peshat* of the verse. This kind of unembellished, contextually grounded interpretation is a distinctive feature of medieval Torah commentary, as we will explore more closely in the pages to come. Interpretation has also evolved well into our day among a third category of expert witnesses, Jewish and non-Jewish scholars, who use even more sophisticated methods, such as the study of ancient Near Eastern languages, anthropology, archaeology, and literary criticism.[10] We will turn to a few of these modern scholars as well in our quest to understand Cain and Abel better.

These experts are not presented in any chronological order; nor do I try to explain their comments in historical context. Furthermore, what I present here is a tiny selection—mere fragments—of their many writings. I imagine them as I believe the Jewish wisdom tradition has always imagined them: leaping off the pages of their commentaries, arguing fiercely with each other and with us across millennia, always alive and always making the Bible come alive.

Indeed, you will soon see that they posit distinct, and often conflicting, perspectives on the case of *Cain v. Abel*. Some of their most imaginative *derash* interpretations may strike you as so remote from a logical explanation as to be ridiculous. Be patient as you read them. Keep in mind that these interpreters are trying to mine a very "barebones" mythic narrative that is not easy to understand, especially in the original Hebrew. Often, their most imaginative rereadings are not intended to uncover the "true" story of Cain and Abel as much as to discover new truths in it that speak to us about being our best and our worst. By joining them in the courtroom, we are joining the

Jewish people—and all people—on a quest to understand who we have become and who we can become.[11]

Cain's trial is our creative midrashic framework for mining the messages and meanings of the Cain and Abel narrative. Before the trial begins, we will read a forensic assessment of Cain's fitness to stand trial—written, I imagine, by the angel, Truth.

We will also be witnesses to a very special deposition (out-of-court interview in which a witness gives sworn evidence to be used at trial in that witness's absence)—of God. God will provide testimony about Cain, Abel, and God's relationship with their family. Together with our expert witnesses' testimony, all of this evidence will help us to understand Cain and Abel's tragic interactions as well as apply their story to our own lives. As interpreters before us have done for millennia, we will hold Cain and Abel's story up to our own faces to see what gets reflected.

Right now, we should turn to Truth's forensic assessment, which attempts to discern if Cain is morally competent to stand trial and be held accountable for his actions.

4

Competent to Stand Trial?

After Cain commits his crime, God interrogates him and accuses him of murdering Abel. Cain tries to deflect God's demand that he take responsibility for his actions, but he is broken under the crushing weight of the evidence — Abel's blood screaming up from the earth.

The court must first consider whether Cain, a murderer whose actions had no precedent in the biblical reading of human history, should even stand trial. Our earlier encounter with the Bible's crime report revealed that it challenges us with more questions than answers, particularly about Cain's moral and behavioral culpability. We could initially ask four difficult questions pertaining to Cain's state of mind at the time of the murder:

1. God warns Cain about struggling successfully with sin. Since Cain has no prior experience with murder and its consequences, how can Cain know what sinful impulses and behavior are?
2. If he does not know what sin is, how can he be held responsible for his behavior, even after God's warning?
3. Before committing murder, is Cain depressed, enraged, or both?
4. Must Cain's state of mind be accounted for in determining his responsibility for what he has done?

American courts of law often turn to mental health experts, specifically forensic psychologists and psychiatrists, to assess the mental fitness of an alleged criminal at the time of a crime. An assessor weighs in on that person's competence to stand trial and helps the court decide the type of sentence or mandated treatment the accused might receive if found guilty. To make appropriate recommendations, he or she considers such factors as family background, earlier traumas, a history of mental illness, and the presence of substance abuse. Underlying this kind of assessment—and our entire justice system—is the assumption that adults are free moral agents who knowingly decide to do what is right or wrong, legal or illegal. However, this assumption can be qualified, even set aside, if it is shown before or during a trial that an alleged criminal's mental state prevented him or her from making a free decision about how to behave.[1]

Faith, Fate, and Forensics

This chapter imagines Cain receiving a different kind of forensic evaluation before trial: a moral health assessment. A significant part of this appraisal involves exploring family dynamics, in the broadest sense of the term.

Upon reviewing the "crime report," we find that Cain's jealous rage and his crime against his brother seem to result more from Cain's being rebuffed by God than by Eve and Adam. First, God seems to reject Cain and his offering in favor of Abel and his offering; then God warns Cain about controlling his sinful impulses; finally, after the crime, God confronts and punishes Cain. Yet shouldn't each of these interventions have been the responsibility of Eve and Adam, Cain's parents, before becoming the task of God, the "Parent"? Eve and Adam's overt absence from the story begs many questions and goads us to fill in the gaps seemingly left by it.

Here, presented to you, is a "forensic" report about Cain's moral competence that addresses this absence. The assessor is the angel named Truth, who we encountered in the introduction, in the story about God's decision to create humanity. Truth, you may recall, argued with God against the creation of people, who Truth feared would do nothing but lie. God's love for humanity and hopes for human potential were so great that God literally threw Truth out of the celestial debate to avoid listening to Truth's counsel. This modern midrash, a sequel of sorts to that story, explores the influence of Eve and Adam's background on Cain and his choices, even though his parents appear to be physically absent during the brothers' fatal conflict.

A Forensic Moral Health Assessment for the Heavenly and Earthly Courts

Defendant: Cain Adamson.

Date of birth: After the expulsion from Eden.

Marital Status: Single.

Race: Human.

Case Number(s): 2.

Related Charges: Murder/fratricide, obstruction of justice.

Current Assessor: Truth, writing the assessment on behalf of the celestial council.

Date of Report: After the expulsion from Eden.

Report Statement, Part I — Comparing Two Crime Reports: In the crime report to this case, the defendant, Mr. Adamson (henceforth known by his first name, Cain) did not explicitly acknowledge that he had committed the crime of fratricide. He initially went on record that he bore no knowledge of Abel's whereabouts and that he was not responsible for his welfare: *"I do not know. Am I my brother's keeper?"* (Gen. 4:9). When, during the interrogation, the lead Investigator, God, confronted him with evidence of the crime, Cain responded ambiguously, *"Gadol avoni min'so,"* as recorded in the crime report.[2] This can be translated, *"My sin is too great to bear,"* an admission of guilt, or "*My punishment* is too great to bear," a reaction to God's pronouncement of Cain's sentence: homelessness and exile. The former interpretation points to Cain's self-incrimination; the latter suggests an insufficient ability to consider his actions beyond his fear of being arrested and punished.

Cain's culpability can also be questioned, given the unprecedented nature of his crime. No one has ever killed another person before him. Lacking any prior example of such behavior and its consequences, is Cain perhaps not competent to stand trial?

Further, the crime report fails to mention Eve and Adam's presence during the brothers' conflict and fatal encounter. Thus, might Cain have lacked sufficient socialization by and warnings from his own parents to allow for the development of his own sound moral judgment? And, if Cain is indeed so deficient, is he in fact culpable for murder?

I assert that such doubts and arguments are unfounded. The crime report notes that God warned Cain, howbeit cryptically, not to succumb to his sinful impulses when he became enraged and depressed at his brother's good fortune of having his offerings accepted by God. Logic demands that we accept that God would not have given Cain this warning, nor entered it into the crime report, had Cain not been morally free to choose otherwise.

However, given the persistence of other experts' doubts about his moral competence, I offer two broader comparisons of records concerning Cain's family history and background. They strongly suggest that (1) Cain was aware of the moral significance of his actions; (2) Cain consciously ignored God's warnings about acting on impulse, implying that he was free not to kill his brother at the time of their conflict; (3) His unjust suffering at the hands of his nuclear family, and even possibly of God, notwithstanding, Cain freely and cruelly murdered his brother, Abel Adamson.

As the reader can see in the table below, the first comparison juxtaposes excerpts from an earlier crime report concerning Cain's parents with excerpts from our current crime report. It underscores well-known, repetitive family behavioral patterns and dysfunctions of which Cain most likely was aware. Note that both records were originally written in Hebrew. I have italicized common phrases in translation. I have also transliterated the original Hebrew, with significant phrases also italicized, to indicate distinctive, echoing similarities between the reports. Certain Hebrew words and phrases will yield different English translations, which are nonetheless similar in meaning.

GENESIS 3:1–24 CRIME REPORT	**GENESIS 4:1–16 CRIME REPORT**
They heard the *sound* [*kol*] of the Lord God moving about in the garden at the breezy time of day; and the man and his wife hid from the Lord God among the trees of the garden (3:8). To Adam God said, "Because you did *as your wife said* [*kol ish-tekha*] and ate of the tree [of knowledge] (3:17).	Then God said to Cain, "*Hark,* [*kol*] your brother's blood cries out to me from the ground!" (4:10).
The Lord God called out to the man and said to him, "*Where are you?* [*Ayeka/*]" (3:9).	*Where is your brother, Abel?* [*Ay Hevel aḥikha?*] (4:9).
When the woman saw that *the tree [of knowledge]* [*ha-da'at*] was good for eating and a delight to the eyes, and that the tree was desirable as a source of wisdom, she took of its fruit and ate. She also gave some to her husband and he ate (3:6). Significantly, the original report repeats variations of the verb "to know" four times.	Cain said, "*I do not know* [*Lo yada'ati*]" (4:9).

God said to Adam ... "*Cursed be the ground [arurah ha-adamah] because of you; By toil you shall eat of it All the days of your life* ... *Until you return to the ground [ha-adamah]*" (3:18–19).	God said to Cain ... "*You shall be more cursed than the ground [arur attah min ha-adamah]*" (4:11).
And the Lord God said to the woman, "*What is this that you have done? [Mah zot asit?]*" (3:13).	God said to Cain, "*What have you done? [Meh asita?]*" (4:10).
And to the woman God said ... "*Your urge [te-shu-ka-tekh] shall be for your husband, And he shall rule over you [Ve-hu yimshol bakh]*" (3:16).	God said to Cain, "*Sin's urge [te-shu-ka-to] shall be for you, But you may be sin's master [Ve-attah timshol bo]*" (4:7).

God gave Eve and Adam explicit warnings about not consuming the fruit of the Tree of Knowledge. Eating the fruit would cause them to possess limitless knowledge like God does. According to the crime report excerpt, Eve recognized the fruit's power, impulsively and freely succumbed to temptation by biting into it, and then gave the fruit to Adam, who also freely ate it. When God confronted Adam with their crime, he passed the blame on to Eve, and she then passed it on to the snake who had initially tempted her (Gen. 3:11–13).

God's sentence for their violation of the law seems to have been preventative. It ensured that they would not impulsively overreach in the Garden again, eating from the Tree of Eternal Life, thereby acquiring immortality, and then becoming divine competitors with God. Thus I assert that Cain's behavioral and character inheritances from his parents include impulse control challenges, defiant oppositional tendencies, and a capacity for avoiding and deflecting blame and responsibility.

The word, phrase, and sound repetitions recorded in both reports have many plausible explanations. For instance, some expert witnesses suggest that most biblical crime records such as ours were originally epic poems that a storyteller recited from memory to an audience. Good storytellers warm up the audience with repeated phrases and ideas that the listeners know from earlier stories, thus stirring listeners to pay rapt attention to the new story and its repeated messages. Employing this storytelling technique, the verbal repetitions in our two crime reports about Adam, Eve, Cain, and Abel establish a close thematic connection between the two reports. Eve and Adam sinned against God because of greed and ambition. Cain sinned against God and his brother because of rage and jealousy. Cain's ordeal intensified that of his parents, but both crimes are bound together by the themes of desire, free moral choice, and responsibility.[3] I submit to the court that during Cain's interrogation, God as lead Investigator warned and interrogated him using this echoing language that would have reminded him of his parents' behavior patterns as well as their experiences within the criminal justice system. It is highly probable that God spoke in such a way to emphasize to Cain that, as difficult as it would be to do, as an adult he could choose not to express the family traits he had inherited or absorbed in the far more drastic circumstances of conflict with his brother.

One outstanding example from the above comparison of the records will suffice for this argument. Part of Eve's sentence for her role in the Tree of Knowledge incident is that her sexual urges will no longer be hers to use at will; her husband will now subjugate her sexually. God's statement here is problematic and troubling, especially given God's previously recorded declaration that men and women are both created equally in God's image (Gen. 1:27).

Nonetheless, let us focus on how God uses this idea metaphorically to describe God's warning to Cain about the power of Sin. Sin, with its powerful desire lurking at the door of Cain's heart, mind, house, behavior, and life, is erotically seductive: It can gradually lure Cain into losing control over his impulses and engaging in grievously destructive behavior. He must maintain deep awareness of his motivations, emotions, and actions at all times. Further comparison of both records reveals a subtle yet significant shift of emphasis in God's warning to Cain. Adam *will* rule over Eve, but Cain *can* rule over Sin. The Hebrew verb *mashal*,[4] "to rule," used in both reports, means, among other things, "will" and "can," connoting fate *and* freedom. God is asking Cain to choose freely to do good. This is very difficult, but not impossible, for him to do.

Eve and Adam are glaringly absent from God's crime report. God noted in the report that they were Cain and Abel's parents and that Eve named her children. A later report, Genesis 4:25, indicates that after the murder they had a third child whom she named Seth. Otherwise, they are not mentioned during the events leading up to and including the murder. I find it highly improbable that these parents neither knew about nor tried to intervene in their children's fatal conflict.[5] Furthermore, Cain's choice of site for the murder, a field far away from human settlement, rather than a place near the family's homestead, suggests that Cain attempted to commit the crime furtively, so as to avoid his parents' active interventions. Even if the record of Cain's life does not include Cain engaging with his parents, we can still assume that they stood alongside God, questioning Cain, "Where is Abel, your brother?"

It has been well established that Cain is, at the very least, his mother's progeny, and the inheritor of his family's legacy. But he is also his own person who must own that legacy as an adult, including when he acts on it for evil. Cain should stand trial because he had ample opportunity to learn from his parents' trials and tribulations—their great errors—well before committing his crime. I submit that God left out Eve and Adam's physical presence from the crime report, even though they were *actually there*. Paradoxically, God did this to underscore their agonizing *moral* presence in Cain's adult life. He needed to accept his responsibilities within his own family, thus providing a supreme model for the broader human family that would come after him. No matter how much God's rejection of him and Abel's elevation over him made him feel wounded and victimized, Cain could not expect his parents to give him cover for his feelings and actions. He could not expect them, God, or society to give him a pass on his moral and legal culpability. Even with his family beside him, Cain needed to stand, as if completely alone, over his brother's body.

In sum, then, Cain's actions are a case study in human beings' stubborn refusal to learn the lessons of their families' pasts.

Report Statement, Part II—Am I My Brother's Keeper?: In part I, I closely compared our crime report with the crime report on Eve and Adam. In part II, I want to suggest that we look closely at Cain's rhetorical question to God, "Am I my brother's keeper?" I believe that it might be the most significant phrase in our crime report, because of its connection with another Hebrew word found in that question: *shomer*, "keeper" or "guardian." To understand the meaning of Cain's response to God, I further analyze Cain's family background based on an even earlier family history record: Genesis, chapter 2.

According to the Genesis 2 report, when Adam was created, God placed him in the Garden of Eden, *l'ovdah u-l'shomrah*, "to work it and to guard it" (Gen. 2:15). The Hebrew word, *l'shomrah*, derives from the same Hebrew verb root as *shomer*, the noun that means a keeper or a guardian. Eve and Adam were entrusted with caring for the Garden of Eden, and thus all physical existence, specifically through farming. It is strange that the first people were charged with this task. Eden was supposed to be an idyllic place where human initiative was unnecessary, given God's creation and watchful care of the Garden.[6] God even told Adam, "From every tree of the garden you may certainly eat" (Gen. 2:15). Why then would Adam be commanded to actively farm and care for it?

I have consulted expert witnesses, whose written testimony for the forthcoming trial provides us with two different approaches to this question. Earlier Rabbis of the Jewish tradition take the view that the working and guarding in this family history record do not refer literally to the actual Garden or to agriculture but, symbolically, to the study of Torah and to the observance of its commandments.[7] This teaching makes a telling moral point. The first people were the founders of humanity, and thus the paradigms for future human behavior at its best and its worst. Although the "real" Eden was lost long ago, Eden continues to be the primary symbol of an ideal world that human beings are always striving to recreate. In this view, Torah—that is, ethical behavior and fear of God—is the basis for achieving this ideal world of peace and harmony between people and within nature. Eve and Adam were, from the beginning, given the sacred task of tending to God's world through proper behavior. Certainly, Cain had the choice to succumb to Sin or to rule over it. Yet the greater purpose of that choice was not to be free to choose in general, but to choose to be the *shomer*, "the guardian," of what God gave his parents. Other analysts of the words *l'ovdah u-l'shomrah* acknowledge this moralistic interpretation but suggest a simpler meaning. I present to the court the testimony of Rabbi Abraham Ibn Ezra,[8] one of the witnesses whose expertise will be presented for the purposes of this trial. He writes: "The meaning of 'to work it' is to cultivate the garden's fruit trees, from which Adam would eat, by watering them. The meaning of 'to guard it' is to protect it from wild animals, by ensuring that they not come in and spoil it."[9]

I contend that Rabbi Ibn Ezra well understands the point the Torah is making when it uses these words to describe the first people's mission from God. God alone could have performed the entire task of guarding and cultivating the world, but God chose not to do so, insisting instead that the first human beings share this responsibility. Thus, Eve and Adam's job as *shomrim*, "guardians," was to work in active partnership with God to keep the world from descending into chaos and lifelessness. I further submit that this call to partnership echoes ironically in Cain's rhetorical question to God during his interrogation. By disavowing himself of all responsibility for Abel as his *shomer*, his "guardian" or "keeper," Cain is alluding to his parents' original responsibility to guard Eden, as God's partners and servants. He then proceeds to distort the meaning of that task, and hence excuse his own actions, in an almost legalistic way: "God, you placed my parents in the Garden of Eden on the condition that they be its *guardians*. Once you forcibly removed them from there, and my family has had to live here beyond Eden's walls, we are no longer responsible for our part of that arrangement. Out here, East of Eden, it is every man for himself. In that circumstance, could You really expect me to be my brother's *guardian* and keeper?"

Cain's renunciation of his role as Abel's *shomer* also points to a corrosive hopelessness in which he has chosen to immerse himself. When the world was new, Cain's parents shared with God a hopeful vision of what human beings would mean for the planet. The first family would coax new life from the materials God gave them for the benefit of all the earth's residents. They had a great mission to be the earth's stewards. When they ate the fruit of the Tree of Knowledge and were expelled from Eden, they traded innocence and safety for mature awareness and deep insecurity. This made continuing the guardian's legacy bestowed on them in Eden even more urgent. Without the benefit of the natural harmonies and built-in resources God had given to them in Eden, they knew they would have added responsibility to actively protect what God gave them, if they wished to survive. As their inheritor of creation, Cain needed to acknowledge that, despite its hardships, his life was a direct continuation of his parents' guardianship.

I submit, however, that ending his brother's life with such ease led Cain to believe that destroying—rather than preserving—life was the more natural default path for him to take. Cain's question, "Am I my brother's keeper?," certainly is a statement of cynicism and a rhetorical disavowal of personal blame. However, it also appears to be his way of despairing: "God, if You made it so easy for me kill my brother, perhaps You never intended for my family and me to care seriously for any living thing in the first place."

As the moral health assessor in this case, I am still quite puzzled. Why did Cain's rage about what he did not get from God, his family, and his life compel him to end the life of his brother? Was Cain's murder of Abel a way of trying to destroy the world, and/or especially himself? It is a cruel and bitter irony that instead of being a source of life on the earth he was supposed to guard, Cain delivered death to the earth by shedding Abel's blood on it. Implicit in Cain's despair-driven rhetorical question, "Am I my brother's keeper?," is God's answer that Cain refused to contemplate and live by: "Yes, Cain, despite everything that hurts you, and whatever you feel about him, you are his keeper."

Report Statement, Part III — Conclusion and Recommendations: Mr. Cain Adamson is morally competent to proceed to trial for the murder of his brother, Abel Adamson. As well, he appears morally competent to learn from his experiences and to teach future progeny about his errors.

I will readily admit that inherent in my outlook is a predisposition toward a very dim view of human beings, God's most ambitious, complex, and fraught project. I voted against the creation of people, and consequently God banished me from the Celestial Council. Cain's fratricide only reinforces my perspective and deepens my fears for humanity's future. Nevertheless, God has insisted on the continuation of the project, God's own possible misgivings notwithstanding.

For humans to be worthy of continued existence and redemption, then, they will need to be held to stringent behavioral expectations. Some — I suggest many — of them will surely not rise to this level of trust, not because they cannot do so, but because they do not want to do so. When their actions betray all that God has entrusted to them — as in the case of murder — they will need to accept God's severest censure, strive to repent for their actions, and make appropriate long-term changes in their behavior. While, in principle, they certainly will be able to engage in these self-correctives, I nevertheless fear that, as Cain's descendants, they will choose not to listen and to change, whether out of laziness, self-righteousness, misplaced despair, or pure egocentrism.

In conclusion, I highly recommend that the court focus its investigations on Cain's motivations for murdering his brother, as well as his capacity to accept responsibility for his crime. Perhaps by doing so, the court will be able to better administer justice and to train humanity to fight its worst impulses and to become better in the process.

5

Interrogating the Interrogator

The following account constitutes the court's first official deposition. The Deponent, God, is being questioned as a witness.[1]

As chief Investigator in the matter of *Cain v. Abel*, God was responsible for the report on Mr. Cain Adamson's criminal activity, as well as for the earlier warning against Mr. Adamson. Due to undisclosed responsibilities elsewhere, God will be unavailable to give testimony at Mr. Adamson's trial; hence, both the prosecuting attorney, Truth, and Mr. Adamson's defense attorney, Lovingkindness, have deposed God. Both depositions specifically concern the matter of Mr. Adamson's murder of his brother, Abel Adamson, on Nisan 14, 0041. Both depositions commence today, on Nisan 17, 0041,[2] with the Prosecuting Attorney, Truth, deposing the Witness first.

A Deposition of God

Truth: Please state Your name.

God: Though I generally go by My standard name, God, my most revealing name is YHVH.[3] It is a combination of the past, present, and future tenses of the Hebrew verb "to be." It means that I am pure being.

Truth: Do You go by any other names or aliases?

God: Some people refer to Me as the Lord, the English version of My name, Adonai.

Truth: Before today, have You ever been deposed, or been asked to offer testimony at a trial or criminal hearing?

God: No, I have not.

Truth: I am going to ask You some questions about Mr. Cain Adamson's murder of his brother, Abel Adamson, which this court needs You to answer. The other lawyers present, Justice, Lovingkindness, and Peace, are allowed to question You if they so choose. Our court reporter is writing down everything we say and will provide us with a transcript. You will have the opportunity to review the transcript for accuracy and to make corrections before you sign it. We also ask You to please let us know immediately if You do not understand a question. Do You understand all this court is asking of You?

God: Your question disturbs Me, as I am used to asking the questions, but, yes, I understand.

Truth: Did You investigate and interrogate Mr. Adamson after his brother's murder?

God: Yes, I confronted him as he stood over Abel's body with a blood-stained stone in his hand.

Truth: Please read through the following record of Mr. Adamson's criminal activity. Did You write this record found in Genesis chapter 4? (*Let the deposition record show that God read the presented crime report.*)

God: Yes, I did.

Truth: Did You interrogate Mr. Adamson's parents at an earlier time, after they were implicated in the Tree of Knowledge case?

God: Yes, I confronted and investigated them as well.

Truth: Now, please read through the following report detailing the criminal activity of Mr. Adamson's parents, Eve and Adam. Did You also write this report, as it is recorded in Genesis chapter 3? (*Let the deposition record show that God read through this second crime report.*)

God: Yes, I wrote it.

Truth: Do both reports accurately reflect Your discussions with these individuals?

God: I wrote verbatim what I discussed with each individual.

Truth: In both cases, did You give the defendants fair warning about their behavior and its consequences?

God: I gave all of them fair warning about their potential behaviors and the consequences.

Truth: A comparison of both records reveals striking similarities between Your warnings to Cain's parents and to Cain. Why did You address the elder and younger Adamsons in such similar ways?

God: To remind Cain of My prior warnings to his family about the necessity for impulse control and obedience to the rule of law. I was all too aware of the multigenerational family dynamic.

Truth: Please tell this Court what events immediately preceded Mr. Adamson's murder of his brother.

God: Cain had recently become religiously pious, and seemed eager to please Me. He prepared Me a sacrificial offering from his rather meager farm produce. Abel then emulated his brother's gesture, offering Me choice animals from his flock. Presented with both of their offerings, I paid attention to Abel and not to Cain. Cain became enraged and murdered Abel.

Truth: If You were personally involved in this case, why didn't You recuse Yourself from this investigation? You have an extensive advisory team, of which the lawyers present are members. Why didn't You arrange for one of the advisory members to investigate Cain?

God: The advisory team is too divided in its opinions about Cain's family for any of the members to have conducted an unbiased investigation.

Truth: Is it perhaps the case that You are too divided about Cain and his family for You to have done so?

Lovingkindness *(rising)*: Objection as to the form of the question. The Deponent's feelings about the defendant and his family are not under investigation.

Truth: Very well. The reporter will note that my question is to be struck from the final transcript. God, do You recall rejecting the findings of Your advisory committee that the Adamson family posed potentially grave dangers to itself and to what would become human society?

Lovingkindness: Once again, objection as to the form of the question. The Deponent's interactions with our advisory committee have no relevance in determining Cain's culpability or sentencing.

Truth: I am concerned about the Deponent's ability to deal objectively with Cain's crime as an Investigator. Counsel certainly recalls that when God asked our celestial advisory council if we felt that human beings should be created, I gave an honest answer that they should not be. Rather than take my analysis into account, God forcibly removed me from the proceedings altogether. This indicates that the Deponent is biased toward the Adamsons as a family.

Lovingkindness: The usual stipulations of a deposition are for questions to establish the facts of the case, not the supposed motives of deponents.

Truth: Let the reporter note that the question and its objection remain in the deposition for now, to be discussed with the Judge before trial.

Truth: Did You issue a warning to Mr. Adamson to refrain from harming his brother?

God: After the brothers' offerings, I noticed Cain's body language. His face muscles were drooping severely, and he appeared both depressed and enraged. I recognized all these as symptoms of his intense need for Me to favor him and his resulting outrage that I had favored Abel. At that point I gave him a verbal warning not to allow his rage and sadness to influence his behavior.

Truth: What did You think was the source of his rage?

God: I surmised at the time that Cain was extremely angry at Me for what he perceived as My favoritism toward his brother.

Truth: Why *did* You reject Cain's offering?

God: I did not reject his offering. That is a common misinterpretation of what I wrote in My report.

Truth: But your report explicitly states that You did so.

God: I did not write that I rejected Cain and his offering. In the original Hebrew transcript I wrote, *"V'el Kayyin v'el minḥato lo sha'ah." Lo sha'ah* means that I was not paying heed—attention—to Cain and his offering. This was because at that moment I was trying to give My undivided attention to Abel—something *he* never received from his parents or his brother.

Truth: Why didn't You explain that to Cain, to clear up any misunderstanding he might have had?

God: I tried, but Cain had already stormed out of My presence.

Truth: Would You please read Your warning to Cain, as You recorded it in writing?

God:

> "Why are you distressed,
> And why is your face fallen?
> Surely, if you do right
> There is uplift.
> But if you do not do right
> Sin couches at the door;
> Its urge is toward you,
> Yet you can be its master." (Gen. 4:6–7)

Truth: Earlier in these proceedings You stated that Your warning to Cain was clear, correct?

God: I did not explicitly warn Cain about Abel, but My warning was clear nonetheless.

Truth: Please explain to us how your warning was clear.

God: I was clear about Cain resisting Sin's influence. Cain needed to consider his rage at his brother in its broader context. Just picture the scene: Cain was so angry, he started kicking down the door to Abel's sheep pen to get at him. Sin was standing *right there*, beckoning to Cain, egging him on, cooing mournfully at him about how Abel was the source of all his troubles. I wasn't being poetic or metaphoric with Cain; I was telling him to be ready to beat Sin to the ground or face wretched consequences. Right then and there, how could he *not* have understood My dire warning that Sin was eager to seduce him into believing that hurting Abel would be an act of self-defense?

Truth: Did You witness Cain Adamson murdering his brother?

God: No, I found Cain standing over Abel's body with a bloody rock. I did not see him commit the murder. It did not matter, though. I knew. . . . I interrogated him, and he confessed: "My sin is too great to bear."[4]

Truth: How do You understood Cain's additional response, which, according to Your report (Gen. 4:14) reads: "Since You have banished me this day from the soil, and I must avoid Your presence and become a restless wanderer on earth, anyone who meets me may kill me!"? Was Cain complaining about being unfairly punished?

God: Absolutely not. He was expressing concern about no longer having My protection, especially given others' desires to avenge Abel's blood.

Truth: It seems odd that Cain would express himself in this manner, since no one else was around to kill him, other than his own parents. Who exactly might have sought to avenge Abel's blood?

God: Besides his parents, any children Eve and Adam might have had later in their lives. By now, Cain was starting to understand from his own experience the long-term effects of intense passion. By killing your victim—actually or even metaphorically—you not only destroy an entire world. You can perpetuate the obliteration of countless other potential worlds through an unending cycle of violence.[5]

Truth: The Prosecution has no more questions for the Deponent. Defense counsel is welcome to cross-examine.

Lovingkindness: Thank you. God, You just testified that Cain was viscerally depressed. He looked enraged, and his facial muscles were drooping severely. Is my understanding of Your testimony correct?

God: Yes, that is exactly what I saw.

Lovingkindness: I am surprised that Your warning to Cain demonstrated no compassion, no understanding, for his suffering.

God: Excuse Me? I spoke directly to Cain about how he was feeling . . .

Lovingkindness: But would You not agree that Your actual words to him might have been taken by him as still more rejection, especially when he was clearly depressed and enraged?

Truth: Objection. Counsel, you cannot question the Deponent about the defendant's purported emotional state, only about the facts of the case as the Deponent saw and recorded them.

Lovingkindness: Counsel, you previously asked the Deponent about the source of Cain's rage. My question is not any different. I am trying to establish the defendant's state of mind prior to the crime, especially given the Deponent's very complex relationship with him and Cain's brother, the victim.

Truth: I'll let the question stand, but we need to remember that this isn't postmortem family therapy; it's a deposition.

Lovingkindness: Thank you, counsel. I'm sure we'll both take that under advisement.

Lovingkindness: God, is it possible that Your question and warning to Cain could have made him angrier and more depressed? After all, You knew he wanted to please You, he was angry and feeling rejected, but You lectured him about doing well and not sinning.

God: My intention was to help Cain see that things would get better for him. His face was literally falling because he was falling emotionally! I told him he could lift himself up, and he would need to keep Sin from dragging him down again. I gave him excellent advice out of deep compassion and concern. It was not a lecture.

Lovingkindness: "It was not a lecture" to Your Divine ears, but what about to his fallible human ears? Again, is it at least possible that Your question and warning to Cain *could* have made him angrier and more depressed?

God: It is possible.

Lovingkindness: You previously testified that Cain's admission, "My sin is too great to bear," confirmed for You that Cain had murdered his brother. Yet when you caught Cain right after the murder, did he plainly admit to the murder?

God: He was evasive, hostile, and defensive. . . . No, he never explicitly admitted to having murdered Abel.

Lovingkindness: How, then, could You—a God who insists on truth and justice—immediately accuse Cain of committing this crime against his brother?

God: It was Abel's scream.

Lovingkindness: Did You hear Abel scream as Cain was allegedly murdering him?

God: No, I heard it after Cain murdered him; really, it was his blood. It was extremely hot that day, and Abel's blood splashed all over the hot ground. It started to sputter, then froth and boil, as it evaporated into a plume of sickening red steam. Have you heard the wheezing or moaning sounds liquids make when they're boiling under a pot? When I heard that, I knew: Abel was wailing.

Lovingkindness: But still, You did not actually see Cain commit the murder.

God: No, but as I said, I knew. The overwhelming evidence was there. Abel's corpse—the first time I ever saw one; the blood-soaked rock in Cain's hands as he stood over his brother; his mouth half agape in stupid, guilty surprise. It was sickening! One of My children could do this . . . ?

Lovingkindness: So, you then questioned Cain as to where Abel was, and when Cain answered that he had no idea and asked if he was his brother's guardian . . .

God: I exploded. The formalities of the murder investigation degenerated into Me throwing Cain up against the wall, begging him to tell Me that he had not done Abel any violence. Bad enough that the boy, My boy, was dead, but by his brother's hand. . . . I pounded his head against that rock in his hand, screaming, "What have you done?"

Lovingkindness: Where were Eve and Adam at this time? You made no mention of them in Your written account.

God: Cain lured Abel into a field on a big hill right outside of Eden. Their parents were where they always were: working on their farm, trying to get their failing crops to grow, well out of sight of their sons' violent encounter.

Lovingkindness: How would You describe Your relationship with the boys?

God: I am their divine Parent. I had asked their human parents to leave Eden before the boys were born. It was better that way for everyone. I had given Eve and Adam freedom, but they abused it, and so I decided I would not let them influence their children. Sure enough, they paid little attention to those boys. I tried to guide Cain and Abel in behaving with fraternal responsibility, if not actual love, but I failed.

Lovingkindness: Let's go back to Your crime report for a moment, as I have further questions.

God: It is not actually a crime report.

Lovingkindness: Then what is it?

God: It is a page from a journal I wrote so that future generations of human beings would remember how much one brother can fail another. I wonder now if writing this journal has also been My way of coming to terms with My own failures as a Parent.

Lovingkindness: Yet this report has all the legal elements of a crime report. You forewarned Cain about not acting on his emotions, and You confronted him after the crime.

God: Of course, I did. I love him. Who else but a parent would lash out like that at a son who had just destroyed his own flesh and blood?

Lovingkindness: So, returning to my earlier question, what was Your warning to Cain if it was not an official criminal warning?

God: It was exactly that — a warning that Cain needed to rein himself in before he did something awful and irreversible. When you love your family, you try to keep them out of trouble. I believed Cain was mature enough to understand My plea without My having to order him: "Do not harm your brother." If I did so, he was liable to experience Me as oppressively overbearing. In any event, we know how well My direct order worked with his equally rebellious parents. So, instead, I was clear about his responsibilities toward Abel in different ways. *Seven* times.[6]

Lovingkindness: Seven times? Please clarify what you mean.

God: I wrote the word "brother" seven times in this entry. Seven times, in seven different ways I tried to tell him, "Abel is your brother; you have to take care of him." Please understand that I always tried to treat Cain as an adult capable of doing right — *even* after I was convinced he had murdered his brother.

Lovingkindness: How did you treat him as an adult in that heated moment?

God: When I asked him, "*Ey Hevel aḥikha?* [Where is your brother, Abel?]" it was meant to confront him in a way that would put him at ease, to give him a chance to confess and repent for his crime.

Lovingkindness: So, when Cain blurted out, "*Gadol avoni min'so,*" was he admitting guilt?

God: He admitted that his sin was too great to bear. Then he began to complain that his punishment would be intolerable and begged Me to forgive him, asking Me rhetorically, "Is my behavior so bad that You cannot bear it?" Then, he dismissed his culpability by asserting, "God, is what I did to Abel so terrible?" Cain was all over the emotional and moral map: contrite and defiant, responsible and self-interested, humble and arrogant.

Lovingkindness: You heard all that from three Hebrew words? Please remember that one man is already dead, and another man's life and freedom depend upon the accuracy of Your testimony.

God: Words carry a lot of nuance and multiple meanings. As I said, Cain was all over the map that day, even if his response to me was clipped.[7]

Lovingkindness: So, Cain understood and admitted what he had allegedly done.
God: Yes, he did.

Lovingkindness: And, as a result, did You grant him clemency or punish him?
God: Yes. Both.

Lovingkindness: Does Cain bear culpability for what he did to Abel?
God: Yes, he does.

Lovingkindness: Do You bear responsibility for what Cain did to Abel?
God: Yes, I do.

Lovingkindness: So, Cain does not bear full culpability for his crime. Is that why You didn't put him to death, but provided him with life-long protection from retribution — essentially handed him a lighter sentence?
God: He deserved death, and I wouldn't ever put him to death. And, maybe, exile was worse than death?

Lovingkindness: I respect Your inscrutability. You are, after all, Master of the universe. Yet, please remember that this Court expects clarity in your responses. You must have handed Cain a lighter sentence for a reason. You had already acknowledged Your own accountability in this matter.
God: I am answering as clearly as I can. Look, My heart exploded from anguish over My murdered son. He deserved better, but I couldn't save him. My heart is also hemorrhaging hate and anger *and* love and sadness for my son the criminal. What else do you expect? This is who my children turned out to be, in great part because I supervised their parents so poorly that

they literally plucked freedom and unbridled power off the Tree of Knowledge. The parents ate from the tree and the children bore poison fruit. Right now, Cain is My only link to the remotest possibility of human survival. This is the cruel and sick paradox of this creation of Mine. If he bears future generations, his internal monsters—hatred, cruelty, murder—are liable to be reborn over and over, again and again. I created these boys, I created their parents, but they aren't clay on a potter's wheel. They've eluded Me since the moment they left My hands, spinning away, spinning away.... What have they done? What have I done? I ... (*The deposition reporter notes that before anyone in the courtroom can intervene, God abruptly ends the deposition and leaves.*)

Commentary on God's Deposition

God moans, barks, like a wounded, angry dog. Then God bolts for the deposition room door, a shock-filled electrical current of disappointment and rage trailing behind.

The beginning was so simple, the creative plan so orderly. God had handed these precious people, Eve and Adam, the simplest of demands and hopes: "Be fertile and increase," "Fill the earth and master it," "Work the Garden and protect it" (Gen. 1:28, 2:15). But impetuous, rebellious Eve and Adam ... they subverted this partnership. And casting them out of Paradise didn't solve the problem; in fact, matters only got much worse. Cain butchered his brother, and the future of humanity tumbled into lawless violence.

God's answer to the angels' deposition subpoena should have been a flat, "divine fiat" No. Who were these wing-clad, self-appointed arbiters of evidence to insist that the Omnipotent Creator and Judge of all existence appear before them to answer their questions? Who were they to pick apart the divine relationship with the Adamsons, and to pore over the intimate details of the Almighty's personal notes?

Who *were* they? They were the ones who had warned God about the wisdom of creating human beings in the first place. Truth, God's "chief angelic officer" as it were, now also prosecuting counsel for Cain's trial, had been insistent then: "Everything You've told us about this new creation is sending warning signals. They'll engage in the most grotesque lawlessness and violence, then they'll lie pathologically to let themselves off the hook. You and we don't need this. Don't bring them into the world!"

But God was bent on the "Human Project," enamored of the Adamsons who would be God's new "children." God had starry visions of what this new family could do, and make, in God's new world. "Truth and his cynicism be damned: people are worth it," God determined. God tossed Truth out of sight of the celestial retinue. Only the other angels' forceful interventions would later convince God to reinstate Truth.[8]

Now, Truth had the gall to depose God! And that deposition was practically not a deposition at all . . . it veered dangerously close to an interrogation, with *God* as the Defendant, and Cain as evidence of divine misjudgment.

How did it all so quickly go wrong? In the dog-eared pages of God's personal journal, the Hebrew word *asah*, meaning "to do" or "to make," stands out in its descent from passage to passage, along with the humans' descent into hell:

Na'aseh Adam b'tzalmeinu. "Let's *make* the human in Our image!" (Gen. 1:27)

Va-yar Elohim et kol asher asah v'hinei tov me'od. "God saw all that God had *made* and found it very good." (Gen 1:31)

Mah zot asit? "God confronted Eve, 'What is this you have *done/ made?*'" (Gen. 3:13)

Meh asita? "God confronted Cain, 'What have you *done/made?*'" (Gen. 4:10)

And later, though (to our knowledge) God hasn't written it yet, as God and humanity reach their darkest point of disillusionment, an anguished cry will pour out from deep within God's shattered heart over the Adamsons' distant offspring. On the eve of their destruction in the Great Flood, God the Parent will come to regret these wicked, violent children God made. Turning on them all (except for Noah, the lone righteous man, and his family), God will wipe them from the earth. Right before all is obliterated, we the jury, the descendants, will read in one last journal entry, God's final cry:

Va-yinaḥem . . . ki asah . . . Va-yitatzev el Libo . . . Niḥamti ki asitim. "The Lord regretted that He had *made* Man on earth, and His heart was saddened. . . . 'I regret that I *made* them.'" (Gen. 6:6–7)

But that is all in the future. Right now, God takes a deep breath and reflects on God's choice to stamp a protective mark upon Cain. That sign tells the world—*he is Mine*—no matter how much he damaged our family. God ponders Cain's punishment of exile, too. No, death would not have been right for this murder . . . not because Cain didn't deserve it, but because *How could I? I love My boy. He killed My other boy. I will not have both of My children dying on the same day.*[9]

Meanwhile, we the jury members are left in the dark. God has vanished. The deposition is over by default, and apparently God will not be at Cain's trial. Since God has expressed that the divine love for Cain continues unabated, why won't God be present to protect God's child? These questions will have to wait. We must now turn to the first day of Cain's actual trial. Cain's testimony awaits us.

Day One of the Trial

On day one of the trial, the court will be calling the following witnesses: (1) Cain; (2) Rabbi ben Uzziel; (3) Rashi; (4) Rabbi Stama, Rabbi Joshua, Rabbi Judah; (5) Rabbi Tanḥuma; (6) Rabbi Eliezer Finkelman. We begin with the testimony of the defendant, Cain Adamson.

Opening Arguments of the Prosecution and Defense

Clerk: All rise. The Celestial Court is now in session, Judge Ne'elam presiding. Please be seated.[1]

Judge Ne'elam (Hebrew for "hidden"): Good morning, ladies and gentlemen. Calling the case of *Cain v. Abel.* Are both sides ready?

Truth: Ready for the People, Your Honor.

Lovingkindness: Ready for the Defense, Your Honor.

Judge Ne'elam: Will the clerk please take the jury's affirmation?

Clerk: Will the jury please stand and raise your right hands? Do each of you affirm that you will fairly try the case before this court, and you will return a true judgment according to the evidence and the instructions of the court?

Jury: We do.

Clerk: Thank you. You may now be seated.

Judge Ne'elam: Before I call on the Prosecution and the Defense to present their opening arguments, I want to speak to you, the jury. As you listen to the testimony of the defendant, his family, and other witnesses, I ask you to recall that Cain has already confessed, as documented in the crime report. However, it is incumbent on you, the jury, to determine if Cain fully understood his potential actions prior to the murder. Also, you are to determine whether Cain confessed out of genuine remorse or in an empty, fabricated gesture to avoid punishment. The Prosecution will please proceed.

Truth *(rising to present the Prosecution's opening statement)*: Thank You, Your Honor. Honored members of the jury, we seek to prove beyond reasonable doubt that the defendant, Cain Adamson, was given fair and sufficient warning by God about controlling his impulses. Further, God would not have issued an initial warning had Cain not been free to follow or reject it. You will hear the testimony of multiple witnesses attesting to these facts. Cain should be sentenced to the maximum extent God's law allows, with no clemency, precisely because he was and is free to choose how to behave. In considering Cain's culpability, you the jury are also asked to consider the ramifications of Cain's behavior and punishment for future generations of the Adamson family, humanity as a whole. What message are we sending to Cain's descendants about the demands of justice and the consequences for wrongdoing if we do not punish Cain to the maximum extent allowed by law? Let us not permit Mr. Adamson to entertain the convenient illusion that he can indulge his most violent impulses without suffering adverse consequences.

Judge Ne'elam: The Defense is welcome to proceed.

Lovingkindness *(rising to present the Defense's opening statement)*: Thank You, Your Honor. Honored members of the jury, we seek to prove beyond reasonable doubt that Cain Adamson's family background and emotional trauma indelibly influenced his decision to murder his brother, Abel Adamson. He was not entirely free to decide the course of his behavior; nor, in any event, was God's warning to him sufficiently clear. Forthcoming testimony from a variety of witnesses will prove that while Cain must be held accountable for his crime, mitigating circumstances must be taken into account when we determine his level of accountability. Cain should be granted clemency to the maximum extent God's law allows, precisely because human freedom to choose is always conditioned by those mitigating circumstances. In granting him clemency, you will also set an important precedent for Cain's descendants, all of humanity, by helping them to balance justice with mercy, as well as punishment with forgiveness and the promise of redemption. Certainly, if Mr. Adamson and his family are free to make good and evil choices, as the Prosecution is arguing, then we are obligated to give him and all of his family the opportunity both to repent for their fallible behavior and to do better in the future.

First Witness of the Day: Cain

Judge Ne'elam: The Prosecution will call its first witness to testify.
Truth: Thank You, Your Honor. I ask the clerk of the court to call the defendant, Cain Adamson, to the witness stand.
Clerk: Mr. Cain Adamson, please rise and approach the witness stand.

(Cain Adamson approaches the clerk of the court.)

Clerk: Please raise your right hand. Do you affirm that you will tell the truth, the whole truth, and nothing but the truth?
Cain: (No response)

Clerk: Mr. Adamson, please raise your right hand.

Cain: (No response)

Clerk: Your Honor, Mr. Adamson seems unable or unwilling to make the affirmation. With your permission, I will forego the affirmation and have the defendant seat himself.

Judge Ne'elam: You have my permission.

Clerk: Mr. Adamson, please be seated.

(Cain is seated. Truth begins the questioning.)

Truth: Are you Cain Adamson, also known as Cain, son of Eve and Adam?

Cain: (No response.)

Truth: Do you acknowledge that you have already confessed to your brother's murder?

Cain: (No response.)

Truth: Mr. Adamson, I remind you that you are the defendant in this trial. We will assume for now that your silence implies your assent. Please tell the court what happened on the date of Nisan 14, 0041, the day you murdered your brother.

Cain: (No response.)

Truth: Why did you and your brother offer gifts to God? Did your parents demand this of you? Were you both trying to appease God? Were you competing with each other?

Cain: (No response.)

Truth: I will ask you a different question. Please describe your emotional state after God rejected your gift. Were you angry? Depressed? Envious of Abel? The crime report suggests all three. In your own words, please tell us how you felt at the time.

Cain: (No response.)

Truth: God warned you about not being ruled by Sin. Had you met Sin before? Did you understand God's warning?

Cain: (No response.)

Truth: What transpired between you and your brother in the field before you committed this crime?

Cain: (No response.)

Truth: When God proceeded to interrogate you, why did you deny knowledge you certainly possessed of your brother's whereabouts? Furthermore, why did you repudiate personal responsibility for your brother?

Cain: (No response.)

Truth: Your Honor, the crime report attests to the fact that the defendant was thoroughly competent to speak with God both before the crime and afterward, during his interrogation. He needs to answer my questions now.

Judge Ne'elam: Mr. Adamson, you are obligated to respond to all questions asked of you. Your silence is obstructing this court's business. I am willing to have you called later, when you are prepared to respond to all the questions posed by this court; otherwise I have no choice but to hold you in contempt of court.

Lovingkindness *(rising to make a request):* Your Honor, with the consent of the Prosecution, we request an opportunity to examine the defendant. We believe we understand what is causing him to be nonresponsive.

Judge Ne'elam: Does the Prosecution consent?

Truth: For now, we do, Your Honor, though we insist on having Mr. Adamson answer our questions in the near future.

Judge Ne'elam: So noted. The Defense may proceed with questioning.

Lovingkindness: Thank you, Your Honor. Mr. Adamson, I recognize this has been a traumatic experience for you and your family.

Are you unable to answer the court's questions because of how you are feeling today?

Cain: (No response.)

Lovingkindness: You have an opportunity to explain to the jury your version of what happened. How did you understand God's warning, as it is recorded in the crime report?

Cain: (No response.)

Lovingkindness: Before your crime, no one had ever committed murder. Did you understand what murder is?

Cain: (No response.)

Lovingkindness: Did you and Abel have a physical altercation? The crime report alludes to a discussion or argument the two of you had right before you killed him. Were you anxious that he might hurt you or kill you?

Cain: (No response.)

Lovingkindness: After God pronounced your punishment, you responded, *"Gadol avoni min'so,"* which could mean "My sin is too great to bear" *or* "My punishment is too great to bear." Were you expressing contrition or protesting the severity of your punishment?

Cain: (No response.)

Lovingkindness: Your Honor, my client appears to be too traumatized to assist in his own defense. The Defense requests that you declare a mistrial, now.

Truth: A mistrial? There is unequivocally no such need. No defendant is legally obligated to speak at his own trial, and you know it. I believe Mr. Adamson is suffering from a severe case of calculating manipulation.

Judge Ne'elam: Enough. I am ordering a recess for consultation and conferral. We will return in three hours.

(The court is hereby reconvened at the order of Judge Ne'elam.)

Judge Ne'elam: Our court is reconvened. Dr. Binah, our court psychiatrist, is prepared to provide us with forensic analysis concerning Mr. Adamson's ability to continue as a witness in his own defense.

Dr. Binah (Hebrew for "discernment"): Thank You, Your Honor. After having conferred with a number of colleagues about Mr. Adamson's sudden loss of speech, I can state with certainty that there is no evidence of physical disability or damage that would have robbed him of his ability to speak. That said, we have discovered hints in the crime report that may explain what has happened to him. Recall God's accusation. Right after Cain denied responsibility for Abel, God confronted him: "Hark, your brother's blood cries out to me from the ground!" Now, recall God's promise. Right after Cain pleaded with God concerning his imminent exile, God said to him, "I promise, if anyone kills Cain, sevenfold vengeance shall be taken on him." God began by speaking *to* Cain, and then suddenly switched to speaking *about* him, in the third person, as if they no longer directly communicated. We surmise that this was the precise moment Cain stopped speaking, and this also corresponds to the inception of Cain's silence in the crime report. As to whether Cain has been silent in this courtroom because he is disabled by genuine trauma or he is being calculatingly coy, we cannot be sure.

Judge Ne'elam: Thank you, Doctor. Mr. Adamson, I am suspicious of your nonresponsiveness, but I have no legal means of forcing you to communicate with us. You have relinquished your opportunity to defend yourself. Are you under the illusion that your best defense is to offer no defense at all, to remain a silent enigma? I do wonder. Mr. Adamson, you may now step down from the witness stand.

(The court notes that Mr. Adamson stepped down from the witness stand and, using hand motions, requested that he be allowed to sit directly in front of his parents. Judge Ne'elam denied his request, citing concerns about family members coaching or agitating the defendant.)

Judge Ne'elam: In keeping with our commitment to freedom of information, we will pause briefly in our proceedings to allow our commentator to explain to the public the significance of this opening of the first day of Mr. Adamson's trial.

Commentary on Cain's Testimony I: Courtroom Poetry

Then God said, "What have you done? Hark! Your
brother's blood cries out to Me from the ground!"
   —Genesis 4:10

Abel's blood was dashed all over the trees and stones.
   —Babylonian Talmud, *Tractate Sanhedrin* 37a

The horror: brother's blood on stones and trees,
Though Cain's one thought is clearing evidence.
He turns away with timeless cruelty.

Their God laments that God has made him free
To cry, "I'm not his keeper," his defense.
The horror: brother's blood on stones and trees.

Our God, appalled, for God can plainly see
Cain does not hear the plaint at his offense,
And turns away with timeless cruelty.

"From earth, your brother's blood cries out to Me.
From this first murder will you learn to sense
The horror: brother's blood on stones and trees?"

Now, in the fall, the ruddy maple trees
Recall Cain's mark and our inheritance:
We turn away with timeless cruelty.

The crimson leaves, they wave Cain's tale at me.
First crime and all its brutal consequence.
The horror: brother's blood on stones and trees.
We turn away with timeless cruelty.
—Dan Ornstein[2]

Coming on Cain standing over the dead body of his brother, God is appalled to discover this consequence of God's bequest of moral freedom. In this first murder scene, the Talmud teaches us, the trees and stones wear the evidence: Abel's splattered blood.

We can imagine that blood having seeped into the deep-red leaves of beautiful Japanese maple trees in fullest color in the fall. The seasonal name, fall, alludes to Eve and Adam's fall from God's favor in Eden, which in turn led to Cain murdering Abel outside the Garden walls. Tying together these disparate elements of chaos and the traumatic effects of the first fratricide are two words: "the horror." These echo the primal phrase "the horror, the horror" in Joseph Conrad's *Heart of Darkness,* a novel that directly confronts the depths of human evil and depravity.[3]

Commentary on Cain's Testimony II: Looking at Cain

On this first day of the trial, we the jury are forced to look at Cain. Not just to confront his evildoing abstractly, but to actually look at him.

Cain shuffles into the courtroom, his ankles shackled, the soil and blood streaking his farm clothes and splotching his calloused hands. His guards push him roughly into his seat at the Defense team's conference table.

Viewing ourselves in the mirror of his sullen, glassy eyes, we mutter, "the horror."

Perhaps, like God, we are appalled by his actions. Perhaps we think, *that fratricidal butcher is not me.*

It takes everyone in court no more than a moment to realize that the crimson stains all over Cain have to be Abel's blood. The Talmud testified that the crime scene was an ugly mess of Abel's blood splattered all over the trees and stones near where he lay lifeless.[4] Obsessed with figuring out how to puncture the life out of his brother, Cain repeatedly stabbed Abel with a sharp rock.[5]

We entertain some sickening thoughts: Cain shares the same blood with his brother that he has spilled; they are, after all, family. Was his crime against Abel a displaced attempt to destroy himself?[6] Was he projecting some kind of blind, homicidal hatred of his parents, even of God, onto Abel?

Our ancestors believed that a murder victim's spilled blood pollutes the earth. Does this mean that, since the first fratricide, the world has literally been poisoned?

Time, and more time, passes. We hear from the prosecuting attorney, the defense attorney, Judge Ne'elam, and the court-appointed psychiatrist, Dr. Binah. You could say we have waited the whole history of humanity to hear directly from Cain as to why he killed his brother. But Cain cannot—or will not—offer us real insight into his crime.

And so, after one last commentary on Cain's testimony, the court will then turn to testimony from our first expert witness, all to better understand what created the world's first murderer.

Commentary on Cain's Testimony III:
What Is in a Name?

> Now the man knew his wife Eve, and she conceived and bore
> Cain, saying, "I have gained a male child with the help of
> the Lord." She then bore his brother Abel. (Gen. 4:1–2a)

Let's begin with Cain's actual name in Hebrew: Kayyin. It is significant, for, in the Bible, names reflect and determine one's destiny.

In our crime report, Cain's mother, Eve, explained her choice of his name as a play on the Hebrew verb *kanah*, "to acquire" or "to create."[7] Just as her husband, Adam, had created her, with God's help (in Genesis 2), she was now truly Ḥavva, in biblical Hebrew the mother of all life, the potent co-creator of a new person with God.

Genesis 3 reports that because Eve and Adam disobeyed God by eating from the Tree of Knowledge, God cursed them and forced them out of the paradise of Eden. Adam and his progeny would forever struggle to sow the land, then to coax food from the hard, mysteriously unyielding earth. Eve and her female offspring would forever be subservient, at least sexually, to the men in their lives, and whenever they gave birth, they would concomitantly experience great suffering and pain.

Traumatized and homeless, the first people figured out how to transcend God's curses. Adam's "seed" could bear the fruit of a new child created in the couple's image and likeness. Eve could cultivate this new life in her body despite the extreme challenges of childbirth. Creating Cain brought Eve tremendous joy and a deep sense of empowerment. The biblical account doesn't relay Adam's feelings, but Eve exults, "I have gained a male child with the help of the Lord!"

Eve would have viewed Cain, her firstborn male child, as the last, best hope. In the legal view of the ancient Near East, this gave him privileged status, including the rights of primogeniture, inheriting the larger portion of his parents' estate.[8] The name she bequeathed him reflected her larger-than-life expectations for him: He would possess the power to create and acquire a new world for her and Adam outside of Eden, in exile.

At the outset, from the moments of the sons' births, Cain was her favorite child. Eve did not even bother to explain Abel's name. Nor did she exult over Abel's arrival. After she had waxed about Cain, "I have gained a male child with the help of the Lord," the text tells us, "She then bore his brother Abel" (Gen. 4:1–2). Abel came into the world already half-forgotten, as we can also gather from his Hebrew name, Hevel, "vapor," a word whose later meaning in the Bible is "vanity" or "meaninglessness."[9]

We might therefore infer that Eve gave Cain the impression that he should think quite highly of himself from an early age, and that he should think little of his brother. Perhaps, from Adam's silence after Cain's birth, we can also infer Adam's disturbing disconnection from his firstborn. Might his mother's ostensible favoritism have contributed to Cain's emotional state at the time of the murder? Might his father's ostensible rejection have also contributed to his decision to murder Abel? Answers to these questions will have to wait as the court calls the first expert witness.

Second Witness of the Day: Rabbi Yonatan ben Uzziel

Clerk: Rabbi Yonatan ben Uzziel, please rise and approach the witness stand.

(Rabbi ben Uzziel approaches the clerk of the court.)

Clerk: Please raise your right hand. Do you affirm that you will tell the truth, the whole truth, and nothing but the truth?

R. ben Uzziel: I do.

Clerk: Please be seated.

(Rabbi ben Uzziel is seated. Truth begins the questioning.)

Truth: Rabbi ben Uzziel, please tell the court about yourself and your expertise in this matter.

R. ben Uzziel: I was the top student of the legendary Rabbi Hillel the Elder, as well as a renowned translator into Aramaic of the prophetic books of the Hebrew Bible. I lived in the Land of Israel in the latter part of the first century BCE and the early part of the first century CE. The actual facts of my life have been swallowed up by time and by the fierce controversies surrounding my translating work. As a lifelong student of midrash, creative Bible interpretation, I succeeded in plunging beneath the plain sense of the prophetic books and sharing the deeper, often exciting new meanings and stories with faithful Aramaic and Hebrew-speaking readers. This threatened everyone. Hillel's colleagues told me to stop writing. I was forbidden to continue my translations of the books of Kethuvim, the last third of the TANAKH (Hebrew Bible). God sent an earthquake and accused me of revealing God's secrets to human beings! That last fact alone should reassure the court that my translations are top-notch; they managed to incur even God's wrath! And I can also promise you that, scholarly protests and consensus to the contrary, the creative translation of the Five Books of Moses "erroneously" attributed to my hand is actually mine . . . every last word and idea.[10]

Truth: We have been told that your interpretive translation of the report about Eve and Adam is considered "radical," even "scandalous." Please explain and elucidate it for us.

R. ben Uzziel: I have concluded that Adam did not initially know his wife sexually. However, he did know that she was desired by, and had relations with, one of God's angels. That angel was Samael, a celestial officer.[11] In short: Adam was not Cain's biological father; Samael was. As for insinuations that this or any of my interpretations are radical or scandalous, I am proud to stand as one link in a very long, illustrious chain of Jews who mine God's words for provocative meanings.

Truth: Your conclusion contradicts the plain sense facts as recorded in the crime report. Quite frankly, it seems rather outlandish. Why would you translate the crime report in such a manner? Haven't you stretched the meaning of its words too far, even distorted them to the point of it's being a new report?

R. ben Uzziel: I stand by my translation. It is true that the opening sentence in the original Hebrew transcript could be translated as follows: "Now the man knew his wife Eve, and she conceived and bore Cain, saying, 'I have gained a male child with the help of the Lord.'" But we can also translate the ambiguous words of that same sentence in the following way: "Now the man knew that his wife was desired by a divine being, and she conceived and bore Cain, saying, 'I have gained a male child together with a divine being.'" This is because the Hebrew verb *y-d-'a* can mean "knowing" cognitively *and* "knowing" in the sense of sexual intimacy. Further, their union makes sense. We know from other early transcripts of that time that divine beings were mating with women and producing angel-human hybrids.[12] This would also explain why Cain, and not Abel, was so highly esteemed in Eve's eyes. Unlike Abel, Cain was semidivine.

Truth: Why would Eve have consented to a union with a divine being when she had Adam, her partner for life, from whose very rib she was formed?

R. ben Uzziel: Adam's utter absence from the naming of the two boys lends strong support to my contention. As we know, Eve's desires and ambitions led her to eat from the Tree of Knowledge and to share its fruit with her husband, after which their paradise was lost. Adam, who had named Eve in Eden after her creation from his rib, was entirely absent from *this* naming. I infer that this is because he was paralyzed by the trauma of expulsion and exile. I have every reason to believe that Eve decided the business of survival in the real world could not wait for him to recover. Eve, as it were, took matters into her own bed, thus ensuring human continuity.

Truth: Inference, even thoughtful inference, is not evidence, Rabbi ben Uzziel. And isn't it true that throughout the years of Jewish biblical interpretation, you have largely been alone in upholding your point of view on the matter?

R. ben Uzziel: It is true that "inference is not evidence," but this interpretation, which you asked for and which I clearly identified as inference, is based squarely on my biblical commentary, which upholds a very high standard of textual proof. While most biblical interpreters have not concurred with my reading of this passage, since when has majority opinion proven to necessarily be the most reliable arbiter of the truth?

Truth: I have no further questions for this witness, Your Honor.

Judge Ne'elam (*turning to the Defense*): Do you wish to question this witness?

Lovingkindness: Yes, Your Honor.

Judge Ne'elam: You may now proceed.

(As Truth returns to the Prosecution team's desk, Lovingkindness rises and proceeds to question the witness.)

Lovingkindness: Rabbi ben Uzziel, based on what you've uncovered in these early reports, what do you believe contributed to Cain's murderous rage at his brother?

R. ben Uzziel: It appears that, given Eve's attitude toward him, Cain knew he could do no wrong in his mother's eyes. To his father, however, he was little more than a reminder of a strained marriage stained by infidelity.

Lovingkindness: How does that help to explain his desire to murder his brother?

R. ben Uzziel: In such a toxic environment, Cain would have done everything he could to please his human father, even going into his backbreaking trade of farming the hard earth. Meanwhile, Adam would have held him at emotional arm's length because he was the result of Eve's affair with Samael. In essence, Cain was suffering for lack of a nurturing father, and emotionally he lacked a brother as well. When God, too—perhaps the ultimate father figure to him—appeared to reject his offering in favor of Abel's offering, the resulting trauma, the double blow as it were, was too much for Mr. Adamson to take. I posit that he displaced his anger and hatred toward Adam and God onto Abel, who was easy to demonize.

Truth (*rising*): Objection, Your Honor, the witness is a Bible scholar and translator, not a forensic psychologist or psychiatrist.

R. ben Uzziel: In the society from which I hail, insight and wisdom concerning people's inner lives come from scholars of biblical wisdom like me.

Truth: Your Honor, I'm happy to have Dr. Binah weigh in on this matter, but the rabbi does not have the therapeutic credentials to do so. Therefore, these suppositions need to be struck from the record.

Judge Ne'elam: I will ask the jury to disregard Rabbi ben Uzziel's last comments for now. However, I will ask Dr. Binah to pursue the witness's claims in greater detail before sentencing, most likely out of court. They are not immediately appropriate for this proceeding, but they are intriguing.

Truth: Thank You, Your Honor.

Lovingkindness: Thank you, Rabbi ben Uzziel. I have no further questions.

Judge Ne'elam: Rabbi ben Uzziel, you may now step down from the witness stand.

(Rabbi ben Uzziel steps down from the witness stand.)

Judge Ne'elam: This court is now adjourned. We will return promptly in one hour to hear the testimony of our second expert witness.

Commentary on Rabbi ben Uzziel's Testimony

Rabbi ben Uzziel's unusual biblical interpretation is certainly open for discussion. It does, however, compel us to consider how Cain's anguish over his father's distance, then absence and even antipathy, may have festered ominously in the background of his relationship with God.

The Defense has attempted to mitigate Cain's culpability, contending that he perpetrated his crime while under severe emotional distress. His mother bore him out of her infidelity; his father treated him dismissively. When God dealt with him, in his perception unjustly, this was the straw that broke the camel's back.

Thus far, the Prosecution has argued that, as God testified in the deposition, God did not treat Cain unjustly. God rightly lavished attention on Abel at the time of the offerings to comfort him for having been treated so poorly by his brother and his parents.

More to the point, the Prosecution is preparing to assert that Abel deserved God's attention because he brought God the very best of his firstlings, whereas Cain did a sloppy, half-hearted job. To elucidate this assertion, the Prosecution now calls one of the most important expert witnesses, Rabbi Shlomo ben Yitzḥak, more popularly known by his Hebrew acronym, Rashi.

Third Witness of the Day: Rashi

Clerk: Rabbi Shlomo ben Yitzḥak, please rise and approach the witness stand.

(Rabbi Shlomo, also known as Rashi, approaches the clerk of the court.)

Clerk: Please raise your right hand. Do you affirm that you will tell the truth, the whole truth, and nothing but the truth?

Rashi: I do.

Clerk: Please be seated.

(Rashi is seated. Truth begins the questioning.)

Truth: Rabbi Shlomo ben Yitzḥak, please tell the court about yourself and your expertise in this matter.

Rashi: I was born in Troyes, France, in the year 1040 CE. I wrote what is considered to be the most popular of all commentaries on almost the entire TANAKH, most notably the Five Books of Moses, as well as the most popular and accessible commentary on almost the entire Talmud. My approach to biblical interpretation is unique in that I focus on *peshat*, the simple contextual meaning of words and phrases, except where I feel that *derash*, the creative meanings of a text taught by my talmudic predecessors, is more adequate. I prefer to be referred to as Rashi, the acronym for my full name, Rabbi Shlomo ben Yitzḥak, or Rabbi Solomon son of Isaac.

Truth: Thank you, Rashi. I am now going to quote from the crime report (Gen. 4:3–5): "In the course of time, Cain brought an offering to the Lord from the fruit of the soil; and Abel, for his part, brought the choicest of the firstlings of his flock. The Lord paid heed to Abel and his offering, but to Cain and his offering He paid no heed." Would you please explain to the court your reading of this evidence?

Rashi: Certainly. The Torah tells us that Cain merely made an offering from the fruit of the ground. That means that Cain offered the worst of what he had, in direct contrast to Abel, who, as the Torah tells us, offered the best of his flock. It seems that Cain, about whom no such reference is made, did not offer his best, but only his leftovers from the harvest.[13] Likely, all he offered were flax seeds. That was not an offering; it was an insult to God and other worshippers.

Truth: Was this what God was implying when, after Cain became depressed and enraged over the rejection of his offering, God said to him, "If you do right, there is uplift"? This is an extremely important but difficult passage to understand.

Rashi: To your question, let me share with the court written evidence from an outstanding expert witness: my predecessor by many centuries, Onkelos, who translated the five books into Aramaic at the direction of two second-century Sages, Rabbi Eliezer and Rabbi Yehoshua. Unlike Rabbi ben Uzziel, Onkelos translated the text quite literally, word for word, rarely taking interpretive license. After carefully reading the crime report, Onkelos explained God's words to Cain thus: "If you improve your behavior, you will be forgiven. If you do not improve your behavior, you will have to account for your sins on judgment day. Repent and you will be forgiven."[14] What else had Cain done up to that point in his life that would garner him this kind of admonition from God? In effect, God was telling Cain to stop moping angrily because of his rejection and to accept responsibility for his own behavior.

Truth: So, this is how Onkelos understands God's warning to Cain about doing right and achieving uplift?

Rashi: Yes, exactly. I would add – and you can corroborate this with him, since we just heard from him in court – that Rabbi ben Uzziel also agrees with Rabbi Onkelos's rendering of this part of the crime report.

(Judge Ne'elam turns to Rabbi ben Uzziel, who has risen and is standing near the witness stand.)

Judge Ne'elam: Rabbi ben Uzziel, do you essentially agree with Onkelos's reading in this section of God's crime report?

R. ben Uzziel: Yes, Your Honor.

Rashi: In general, both translators take different approaches to reading this crime report, but they are both trustworthy expert witnesses, and they agree on the matter of this specific translation.

Truth: The Prosecution has no more questions for this witness, Your Honor.

Judge: Would the Defense like to cross-examine the witness?

(As Truth returns to the Prosecution team's desk, Lovingkindness rises and proceeds to question the witness.)

Lovingkindness: Thank You, Your Honor. Rashi, would you agree that, your interpretations notwithstanding, God's admonition to Cain in the crime report is not entirely clear on first reading?

Rashi: It is ambiguous, I would agree.

Lovingkindness: This might allow for a different reading of God's warning, correct? For example, perhaps God was not criticizing Cain for his poor offering, but warning him that his anger and sadness at being dealt with poorly by God would lead him to evil behavior, correct?

Rashi: I am not sure I am comfortable with what you are implying about God.

Lovingkindness: With all due respect, your discomfort is not of relevance to this court. Are you not, in one sense, looking to exonerate God for possibly making an arbitrary choice between the brothers' offerings?

Truth *(rising)*: Objection, Your Honor, God is not on trial here; Cain is.

Judge: Objection sustained.

Lovingkindness: Rashi, while my client does seem to have offered God an inadequate offering, is there not conflicting evidence about Cain's motivations at the time? Can you confirm with absolute certainty that he did this with malevolent intent?

Rashi: I am not sure I understand your question.

Lovingkindness: Is it possible that Cain took on his father Adam's business of farming, perhaps to please his father, and he was constantly humiliated by poor crop yields?

Truth: Objection, Your Honor, counsel is speculating as to the Defendant's state of mind in making a business decision many years ago. Further, the line of questioning is a non sequitur.

Lovingkindness: Your Honor, I am determining Mr. Adamson's persistent state of mind at the time of the crime by establishing motive at the time of the sacrificial offering.

Judge: Objection overruled. The Defense will continue.

Lovingkindness: Rashi, we have written evidence that, prior to the expulsion from Eden, God cursed Cain's father Adam for his role in eating the forbidden fruit of the Tree of Knowledge of Good and Evil. Would you please read this earlier piece of evidence to the court?

Rashi (*reading from the section of the crime report about the defendant's parents, otherwise known as* Gen. 3:17–19):

>Cursed be the ground because of you;
>By toil you shall eat of it
>All the days of your life:
>Thorns and thistles shall it sprout for you.
>But your food shall be the grasses of the field;
>By the sweat of your brow
>Shall you get bread to eat.

Lovingkindness: Rashi, is it possible that Cain proffered poor offerings not because he lacked concern or he was disrespectful to God, but because he inherited his father's curse and he was doomed to farm poorly?

Rashi: It is possible.

Lovingkindness: Is it possible that my client could only offer what the ground gave him, which was not much?

Rashi: Yes, I suppose that is possible.

Lovingkindness: And thus, isn't it also possible that, even if Cain was his mother's favored child, he still desperately wanted to make his father—and ultimately, in Adam's absence, God—proud of him?

Rashi: It's possible, but not probable. The crime report details the extent to which Abel went in giving his offering. The report does not correspondingly tell us that Cain went to such—or indeed any—lengths to please God. From this we can reasonably infer that Cain's attitude was vastly different than Abel's.

Lovingkindness: But it is possible, correct?

Rashi: Yes, it is possible.

Lovingkindness: Is it possible that my client did not offer God a scanty offering on purpose—in fact, that he made his offering that day in a state of fearful anticipation of failure, which is why "he was much distressed and his face fell"? Wouldn't fulfillment of his worst fear—being ignored by God—equally explain Cain's anger and depression?[15]

Rashi: Again, what you are saying is all possible but not probable. God is unconditionally just and would never have treated Cain so arbitrarily for something over which he had no control.

Lovingkindness: I would suggest, rabbi, that you are basing your view of God's justice on your own religious beliefs and biases, and not on the evidence in the crime report. Your Honor, I have no more questions for this witness.

Judge Ne'elam: Rashi, you may now step down from the witness stand.

(Rashi steps down from the witness stand.)

Judge Ne'elam: This court is now adjourned. We will return promptly in one hour to hear the testimony of our next expert witnesses.

Commentary on Rashi's Testimony

In its opening statement, the Prosecution argued that, Cain's state of mind notwithstanding, God's address to him after the rejected offering was a formal warning, based on Cain's full ability to make morally free choices about his behavior:

"Why are you distressed,
And why is your face fallen?
Surely, if you do right
There is uplift.
But if you do not do right
Sin couches at the door;
Its urge is toward you,
Yet you can be its master." (Gen. 4:6–7)

From the Prosecution's point of view, the emotional reasons underlying Cain's behavior are irrelevant. All we need to know in judging Cain is that God warned him about wrongdoing and that he chose to commit bloodshed regardless. However obtuse the details of God's warning to Cain, the warning itself is also a reminder that Cain was completely free to choose how he would react to disappointment and frustration.

The Defense argued quite differently in its opening statement. God never directly warned Cain against doing Abel harm; nor did God explicitly threaten Cain with punishment for such behavior. Indeed, Cain was never served any kind of legitimate notice about the consequences of harming his brother. God never warned him not to take the life of another person. The warning Cain received was too vague to possess the force of law, and, moreover, could be interpreted in many other ways. Certainly, God did warn Cain to exhibit control over his feelings, but perhaps God was instructing Cain not to offer improper sacrificial offerings, Cain's dark and ambivalent feelings about God, his parents, and his brother notwithstanding. Or, perhaps God was comforting Cain, reassuring him that once he behaved better, his fallen face would be uplifted.

Further, how could Cain, the third person born into the world, be expected to refrain from committing murder, when he had no precedents for knowing what murder was, that it was wrong, and that doing it would subject him to punishment? No evidence has yet pointed to Cain acting out of premeditated malice. At the very most, we can say that Cain committed a crime of passion in the heat of an angry exchange with his brother, fueled by his humiliation, depression, and perhaps even fear of his brother. How, then, could he be fully liable for his actions, their severity notwithstanding?

The Prosecution has held that since God did warn Cain about resisting Sin, the fact that Cain knew nothing specifically about murder is irrelevant. Cain knew enough from his family's background and from God's warning to surmise that he should keep his hands off his brother.

At the very least, Rashi's expert testimony raises the possibility that God's rejection of Cain's offering was justified and that Cain's angry response to that rejection was not. At the same time, however, Rashi's explanation for Cain's offering—that Cain merely offered poor produce—leads us to make a very uncomfortable inference. Our knowledge that God cursed Adam's farming endeavors before Cain and Abel were born compels us to at least ask: Isn't it possible that Farmer Cain's poor offering resulted from haplessness and misfortune rather than dismissiveness? In other words, might Cain have given the very best offering he could, considering the preordained circumstances? Cain's absolute culpability for murdering Abel notwithstanding, might this wider context of interpretation give us pause to sympathize with Cain more deeply? Is it possible that, in the brothers' competitive contest of offerings, God set Cain up to fail?

Moving forward with the case, the court will proceed to explore the brothers' last exchange before Cain murdered his brother. To address precisely what Cain said to Abel in the field—another gap in the crime report—Truth has called to the stand three expert witnesses from the ancient Land of Israel: Rabbi Stama, Rabbi Joshua, and Rabbi Judah. For the sake of simplicity, our transcript has compressed all three testimonies into one.

Fourth Witnesses of the Day: Rabbi Stama, Rabbi Joshua, and Rabbi Judah

Clerk: Rabbi Stama, Rabbi Joshua, and Rabbi Judah, please rise and approach the witness stand.

(Rabbi Stama, Rabbi Joshua, and Rabbi Judah all approach the clerk of the court.)

Clerk: Please raise your right hands. Do you affirm that you will tell the truth, the whole truth, and nothing but the truth?

Rabbis: We do.

Clerk: Please be seated.

(The witnesses are seated. Truth begins the questioning.)

Truth: Rabbis, please tell the court about yourselves and your expertise in this matter.

Rabbi Stama: Stama is not my actual name, but my nickname, meaning, "Anonymous one." Think of me as a spokesperson for the majority of the ancient Sages, sort of a talmudic version of "You know what they say . . ."

Rabbi Joshua: I am Rabbi Joshua from Sikhnin, a town in the lower Galilee region of the Land of Israel. I lived in the latter part of the third century CE. A student of the renowned Rabbi Levi, I specialized in *midrash aggadah*, exegesis and interpretation of the nonlegal portions of the Bible.

Rabbi Judah: I am Rabbi Judah bar Ami, the son of the renowned Rabbi Ami. I lived in the city of Tiberias in the Land of Israel in the earlier part of the third century CE. I also specialized in *midrash aggadah*.

Truth: According to the crime report (Gen. 4:8): "Cain said to his brother Abel . . . and when they were in the field, Cain set upon his brother Abel and killed him." Their dialogue is entirely missing from the report. Rabbi Stama, based on your examination of the evidence, can you determine for us what Cain actually said to Abel just before the murder?

Rabbi Stama: A fatal argument between the brothers ensued after Cain and Abel agreed to divide up the world. Cain, the farmer, took over everything connected to landed property. Abel, the shepherd who was always on the move with his flocks, took over everything connected to moveable property. Cain said, "That land on which you are standing, where your sheep graze, is mine! Get off of it!" Abel said, "That clothing you are wearing, which is made of wool, is mine. Take it off!" Their argument became so heated that Cain rose up and murdered Abel.

Truth: On what evidence do you base this conclusion?

Rabbi Stama: On a close reading of the beginning of the crime report. God, the Chief Investigator, generally writes in a highly laconic style. God would not have wasted words in the introduction to let us know that Cain was a tiller of the ground and Abel was a shepherd. We could have easily inferred this from the brothers' respective offerings. Even if we didn't infer this, letting us know the brothers' respective professions would have been irrelevant unless God was implying something specific and revealing—in this case, the manner in which Cain and Abel each jealously guarded their literal and professional turf. This ultimately led to the shedding of blood.

Truth: Rabbi Joshua, please give us your explanation of what happened between the brothers.

Rabbi Joshua: I agree that Cain and Abel had divided all of the landed and moveable property evenly between them, but that was not in and of itself the source of their dispute. Rather, they were arguing about whose territory would later house the Holy Temple of Jerusalem. They were essentially arguing over religious supremacy.

Truth: On what evidence have you based *your* conclusion?

Rabbi Joshua: According to the crime report, the brothers were in a field during the murder. The Hebrew word for field, *sadeh*, often alludes to Mount Moriah in Jerusalem, where the Holy Temple would later be built. So, they were arguing about who owned the very land they were standing on, which they sensed would later become sacred ground. As textual proof, I refer you to the words of the biblical prophet Micah: "Zion shall be ploughed as a field, / And Jerusalem shall become heaps of ruins, / And the Temple Mount / a shrine in the woods" (Mic. 3:12). Zion, the holy city, and the Temple Mount are all parallel to one another in this passage; they all refer to the same thing, and Micah tells us they will all be found in a field. Ultimately, though, I think Cain and Abel were arguing over something even bigger than this. They came to blows over who was worthier to host God's Holy Presence — in other words, whose religious devotion was more acceptable to the Creator. This is the kind of argument that never turns out well.

Truth: Rabbi Judah, please explain to the court your interpretation of the argument.

Rabbi Judah: I am convinced that Cain and Abel were arguing over who would get to have sex with the women in their community.[16]

Truth: How do you read *that* from the crime report?

Rabbi Judah: Your Honor, I do ask your forgiveness and that of the court for the indelicacy and seeming prurience of my testimony. To be more specific, it is my contention that, in the absence of other women, the brothers were fighting over sexual conquest of their mother, Eve. With no other access to sexual partners at that earliest time in human history, and no rules yet in existence to curb their worst interpersonal behavior and impulses, the brothers engaged in mortal battle egged on by their desires. The tragedy is that they could have expended that energy civilizing those desires.

Judge Ne'elam: Rabbi Judah, I think this court can forgive the indelicacy; I'm just not sure it can forgive the seeming preposterousness of your claim. How could your reading of the crime report bring you to this conclusion?

Rabbi Judah: Your Honor, I admit up front that the textual basis of my claim is flimsy. However, the logical and psychological bases are not. Given the raw power of unchecked sexuality, it stands to reason that sexual competition, no less than material gain or religious animosity, would have incited the brothers' conflict.

Truth: Thank you, Rabbis Stama, Joshua, and Judah. Together all three of you have proffered explanations of Cain's motives prior to the murder: Cain's acquisitive, religious, or sexual jealousies. Regardless of your specific arguments, would you agree that Cain was certainly aware of his overwhelming feelings of jealousy and hostility, as God had already addressed these concerns with Cain? Would you concur that, however emotional the circumstances that upset Cain, reasonable, civilized persons nonetheless have the capacity to monitor their impulses to violence?

Lovingkindness *(rising)*: Objection, Your Honor, the Prosecution is leading the witnesses. The witnesses are experts in interpreting the incident in the crime report, not determining how we would expect Cain to respond.

Judge Ne'elam: Objection sustained, and if the Prosecution has no further questions for the witnesses, the Defense may cross-examine them.

Truth: We have concluded questioning these witnesses, Your Honor.

Lovingkindness *(approaches the witness stand)*: Thank You, Your Honor. Rabbis, based on your testimony, would you conclude that Abel was just as prone to acquisitive, religious, or sexual jealousies as was Cain? In your estimation, was Abel as passive as the crime report presents him, or was he in active conflict with his brother prior to the murder?

Rabbi Stama: With the court's permission, I'll address both questions on behalf of my colleagues. We believe that Abel was just as prone to those jealousies as Cain and that Abel was in active conflict with him prior to the murder.

Lovingkindness: I have no further questions, Your Honor. Your Honor, at this time, the Defense wishes to call Rabbi Yonatan ben Uzziel back to the witness stand for his testimony regarding Cain and Abel's conversation in the field.

Judge Ne'elam: Rabbi Stama, Rabbi Joshua, and Rabbi Judah, you may now step down from the witness stand.

(Rabbi Stama, Rabbi Joshua, and Rabbi Judah step down from the witness stand.)

Second Witness Rabbi Yonatan ben Uzziel Returns to the Stand

Judge: The Defense may now call its witness.

Lovingkindness: The Defense calls Rabbi Yonatan ben Uzziel back to the witness stand.

(Rabbi ben Uzziel rises again from his seat in the courtroom and returns to the witness stand.)

Lovingkindness: Rabbi ben Uzziel, what, in your scholarly estimation, did Cain say to Abel before he murdered him?

R. ben Uzziel: I contend that when they were in the open field, Cain said to Abel, "I can see that the world was created with mercy, but that a person's good deeds do not bear the fruit of reward. God plays favorites. For why else did God accept your offering with pleasure but reject mine?" Abel replied, "I completely disagree with you! My offering was simply better than yours." Cain then answered Abel, "There is no justice, there is no divine

Judge, there is no reward in the afterlife, and the righteous do not receive a reward for being good." Abel replied, "You are absolutely wrong on all of your points!" They began to argue fiercely, whereupon Cain smashed in Abel's head with a rock and killed him.[17]

Lovingkindness: Thank you, Rabbi ben Uzziel. So, if I understand your testimony correctly, Cain's grievance could have been justified, at least in his own mind. He offered the best he could, given the meager circumstances of his profession. Cain was so wounded by God's rebuff, real or perceived, that he interpreted it nihilistically: God was unfair to him specifically because God's ongoing plan for the universe is thoroughly unjust. Cain's anguish and despair at his discovery was so intense he turned it outward, expressing it as murderous rage against Abel.

R. ben Uzziel: That is correct. I would only add that my interpretation of this gap in our crime report is not mere speculation. I base it on credible textual evidence that I have gathered from the forensic report written and delivered by Truth, lead counsel for the Prosecution.

Truth (rising): Objection, Your Honor, it is highly inappropriate for this witness to twist my words in order to defend Mr. Abelson.

Judge Ne'elam: Counsel, if the witness can provide credible evidence of his claim based on your report, I have to allow it. Rabbi, this had better be well-developed proof.

R. ben Uzziel: Your Honor, please allow me to quote directly from the forensic report: "Cain's renunciation of his role as Abel's *shomer* (guardian) also points to a corrosive hopelessness in which he has chosen to immerse himself. When the world was new, Cain's parents shared with God a hopeful vision of what human beings would mean for the planet. The first family would coax new life from the materials God gave them for the benefit of all the earth's residents. They had a great mission: to be the earth's stewards. When they ate the fruit of the Tree of

Knowledge and were expelled from Eden, they traded innocence and safety for mature awareness and deep insecurity. This made continuing the guardian's legacy bestowed on them in Eden even more urgent: Without the benefit of the natural harmonies and built-in resources God had given to them in Eden, they knew they would have added responsibility to actively protect what God gave them, if they wished to survive. As the inheritor of creation, Cain needed to acknowledge that, despite its hardships, his life was a direct continuation of his parents' guardianship. I submit, however, that ending his brother's life with such ease led Cain to believe that destroying—rather than preserving— life was the more natural default path for him to take. Cain's question, 'Am I my brother's keeper?' certainly is a statement of cynicism and a rhetorical disavowal of personal blame. However, it also appears to be his way of despairing, 'God, if You made it so easy for me to kill my brother, perhaps You never intended for my family and me to care seriously for any living thing in the first place.'" This is a direct quote from Truth, who now leads the Prosecution, Your Honor. *He asserted that Cain's despair drove him to evil. I only reconfirmed it.*

Judge Ne'elam: Does the Prosecution wish to cross-examine the witness?

Truth: No, Your Honor.

Judge Ne'elam: Rabbi ben Uzziel, you may now step down from the witness stand.

(Rabbi ben Uzziel steps down from the witness stand.)

Commentary on the Testimonies of Rabbis Stama, Joshua, Judah, and ben Uzziel

A textual gap like Cain's missing dialogue with Abel in the killing field is irresistible to the Rabbinic Sages, for whom every gap and grammatical anomaly is a literary, spiritual, and moral gold mine begging to be excavated. What did Cain possibly say to Abel in the field before the murder? If we could know this, could we perhaps place the horror of his actions in some larger, more meaningful, context? Some ancient translations outside of Rabbinic literature, such as the Syriac Peshitta and the Greek Septuagint, supply us with the simplest explanation: Cain said to Abel, "Let's go into the field." It makes so much sense, and the implications of its simplicity are devastating: Cain plotted the murder in cold blood, which is why he lured his own brother into a field where he could do away with him out of the sight of their parents. Without a sense of familial responsibility toward others, we humans will use our extraordinary intelligence and strategic sophistication to engage in barbarity.

Rabbis Stama, Joshua, and Judah would not necessarily disagree with this perspective, but they explain it in more excruciating detail. What motivates us to engage in such barbarity toward our brothers and sisters? An elemental jealousy impels us to eliminate them when we feel threatened by their encroachment on us and our well-being. As we learn during Rabbi Tanḥuma's and Sin's upcoming testimonies, Cain fell into the trap of believing that Abel was victimizing him, and that he was justified in destroying him in self-defense, particularly to protect his property, his religious preeminence, and his sexual security.

Rabbi ben Uzziel's testimony could be interpreted as making God "the Villain" in our story. This viewpoint has little explicit support in the text, and no support in the later commentaries. Nonetheless, his testimony is remarkable because it gives Cain the sympathetic voice of a man who felt unjustly abused and despondent about life.

Rabbi ben Uzziel is able to paint Cain with a different brush because our story is just vague enough to allow for a radical interpretation. Most importantly, by giving Cain room to lament the unfairness of his life and to consequently infer God's arbitrariness, Rabbi ben Uzziel opens up another possible meaning of God's warning to Cain and to us, as we see below.[18]

By now, Cain is trembling in his seat, still refusing or unable to speak. It remains unclear whether Cain's hot-blooded crime of passion was motivated by an arrogant sense of privilege or by a desperate sense of having been abused and rejected. How Cain responded when God called him on his actions could shed light on this mystery.

Focusing on this evidence, the Prosecution proceeds to call an early midrashic commentator, Rabbi Tanḥuma, to the stand.

Fifth Witness of the Day: Rabbi Tanḥuma

Clerk: Rabbi Tanḥuma, please rise and approach the witness stand.

(Rabbi Tanḥuma approaches the clerk of the court.)

Clerk: Please raise your right hand. Do you affirm that you will tell the truth, the whole truth, and nothing but the truth?

Rabbi Tanḥuma: I do.

Clerk: Please be seated.

(Rabbi Tanḥuma is seated. Truth begins the questioning.)

Truth: Rabbi Tanḥuma, please tell the court about yourself and your expertise in this matter.

Rabbi Tanḥuma: My full name is Rabbi Tanḥuma bar Abba. I lived in the fourth century CE in the Land of Israel, where I achieved renown as a midrashic scholar and compiled an authoritative collection of midrashic teachings on the Bible. I also beat the local Roman governor in a contest of wits, so he had me thrown in a pit of wild animals as punishment. Miraculously, I survived.[19]

Truth: We appreciate your having survived so that you could be with us here today, rabbi. I am going to read aloud the text of the crime report (Gen. 4:9–10): *The Lord said to Cain, "Where is your brother Abel?" And he said, "I do not know. Am I my brother's keeper?"*[20] *Then God said, "What have you done? Hark, your brother's blood cries out to me from the ground!"*[21] Based on your midrashic analysis, please explain to the court what you think Cain meant when he said, "Am I my brother's keeper?"

Rabbi Tanḥuma: What he meant was, "You, God, are the Keeper of all living things, yet You are demanding of me that I account for Abel's whereabouts? Yes, I killed him, but you created the impulse to do evil within me, which made me commit the crime. If You are the Keeper of all living things, why did You not stop me from killing him? *You* were the One who killed him, for if you had not rejected my offering, I would never have gotten jealous of him in the first place."[22]

Truth: How did you arrive at this conclusion?

Rabbi Tanḥuma: My task is not only to read the plain words of this crime report but to hear them as well: their emotional tone, moral valence, and possible messages hidden underneath. As my colleague Rabbi Stama just testified, God's writing style is highly laconic, and I would also say it is highly suggestive. The way the Chief Investigator reported Cain's response, it suggests evasiveness and cynicism on Cain's part. Whether Cain actually said, "Am I my brother's keeper?" or God paraphrased him, the rhetorical question appears fraught with a callousness that cannot be ignored.

Truth: I have no more questions for this witness, Your Honor.

Judge Ne'elam: Does the Defense wish to cross-examine the witness?

Lovingkindness: No, Your Honor.

Judge Ne'elam: Rabbi Tanḥuma, you may step down from the witness
stand.

(Rabbi Tanḥuma steps down from the witness stand.)

Commentary on Rabbi Tanḥuma's Testimony and Cain's Response to God

In Rabbi Tanḥuma's view, Cain's answer to God went a very ugly step
beyond his mere refusal to take responsibility for his brother. Cain
rationalized his behavior by turning himself into the victim, God into
the perpetrator, and Abel into the unfortunate by-product of God's
criminal negligence as Creator and Ruler. Asserting that God gave
him the impulse to do evil, also known as *yetzer ha-ra*, Cain divested
himself of any culpability for his crime. He presented the murder as
simultaneously an act beyond his control and an act taken in self-
defense. He, not his victim, was the aggrieved party.

Rabbi Tanḥuma's reading of Cain's response to God has very disturbing implications for the broader matter at issue in our trial, God's
argument with the angels that we encountered previously. Given
our equal capacity for lying and violence, as well as for compassion
and justice, was it worth it for God to have created human beings
in the first place? If Rabbi Tanḥuma's description of Cain's almost
sociopathic callousness is accurate, the Prosecution has reasonable
grounds to argue against humanity's future capacity for personal
responsibility and repentance. This is because, while Cain might not
represent every person in toto, he certainly symbolizes every person's
potential, and that potential seems not worth the suffering it would
engender. Yet what if our expert witness has overinterpreted Cain's
words? Cain's response to God—"Am I my brother's keeper?"—is certainly no expression of remorse or acknowledgment of culpability;
quite the opposite. However, it is also not necessarily an expression

of calculated malice. We the jury might imagine these words pouring defensively out of the mouth of this angry, disgruntled young man who is confronted with the truth of his murderously impetuous behavior by God, truth's source. Terrified by what he has done to Abel in that moment of dark passion, Cain does what any guilty person confronted by the authorities would do: He dissembles in a manner that allows him to come clean without having to admit directly what he did.

"I do not know. Am I my brother's keeper?" One way we the jury can ascertain whether these words indicate that Cain is remorseful or recalcitrant is to revisit his three-word Hebrew response to God, whose accurate translation remains stubbornly elusive: "*Gadol avoni min'so.*" Is the contrite Cain admitting to God, "My sin is too great to bear," or is the defensive Cain complaining to God, "My punishment will be too great to bear?" Again, knowing whether or not Cain repented sincerely when confronted by God could have important implications for how all of humankind might be viewed. Are we capable of genuinely seeking forgiveness for wrongdoing, and of trying to be better people? Do we simply "repent for show," to avoid trouble and ingratiate ourselves with others and with God? Do we acknowledge when we have behaved badly, or are we incapable of this level of introspection? In the quest to finally decipher the meaning of these three words, the Prosecution calls Rabbi Eliezer Finkelman, a contemporary expert witness, to the stand.

Final Witness of the Day: Rabbi Eliezer Finkelman

Clerk: Rabbi Finkelman, please rise and approach the witness stand.

(Rabbi Finkelman approaches the clerk of the court.)

Clerk: Please raise your right hand. Do you affirm that you will tell the truth, the whole truth, and nothing but the truth?
Rabbi Finkelman: I do.

Clerk: Please be seated.

(Rabbi Finkelman is seated. Truth begins the questioning.)

Truth: Rabbi Finkelman, please tell the court about yourself and your expertise in this matter.

Rabbi Finkelman: I teach literature and composition at Lawrence Technological University in Southfield, Michigan, and share responsibilities as co-rabbi of Congregation Or Chadash in Oak Park. I earned a PhD in comparative literature at the City University of New York, and rabbinic ordination at the Rabbi Isaac Elchanan Theological Seminary of Yeshiva University. In my essay "Cain's Im(penitent) Response to His Punishment," I have summarized eight nuanced ways in which the talmudic Sages and later commentators have read Cain's three-word confession, based on ambiguities of translation and tone. I follow earlier midrashic teachers in suggesting these eight readings.

Truth: What are these eight readings?

Rabbi Finkelman: Cain could be:

1. penitent of his sin;
2. impenitent, though regretful of his punishment;
3. despairing of God's forgiveness,
4. despairing of God's clemency;
5. penitent, yet unsure of his ability to live with his guilt;
6. penitent and trusting in God's merciful clemency;
7. unsure of his ability to live with his punishment;
8. impenitent and arrogantly certain that God will forgive and grant clemency.

Truth: This is a staggering number of possible interpretations of three words. Which one is correct?

Rabbi Finkelman: As I have written elsewhere, "Depending upon which reading we choose, Cain may already be a sinner or planning to become one. Alternatively, he is merely a jealous older brother, or even a frustrated adolescent unused to failure. Perhaps we do not need to pick only one reading, but can keep multiple options in mind when trying to understand Cain. . . . Seeing Cain as an unrepentant evil doer is a defensible reading of the text. However, so is a reading that presents Cain as remorseful and tortured by his behavior."[23]

Truth: So, in your expert opinion, there is likelihood that, after God confronted him, Cain fully understood the seriousness of what he had done to his brother?

Rabbi Finkelman: There is certainly that likelihood.

Judge Ne'elam: Rabbi, I want to step into this examination for a moment. Are you saying that Cain's response to God was thoroughly ambiguous and that God merely recorded what Cain said; or that God—inexplicably I might add—purposely recorded Cain's words with no explanation in order, perhaps, to maintain ambiguity and multiple interpretations?

Rabbi Finkelman: I do not presume to know Cain's intentions or God's mind. What is clear to me, as was clear to earlier expert witnesses, is that evidence about Cain's behavior and intentions is not open and shut. We know that the defendant murdered his brother. He did a horrible thing. Does that fact tell us everything we need to know about him, about his capacity for self-honesty and repentance? I don't believe so. Since Cain refuses to or can't speak with us, we have only the crime report and our own interpretive insights to rely on for answers.

Judge Ne'elam: Does the Prosecution have any further questions for the witness?

Truth: No, Your Honor.

Judge Ne'elam: Does the Defense wish to cross-examine the witness?

Lovingkindness: No, Your Honor, though I wish to emphasize to the jury and to you the critical relevance of Rabbi Finkelman's testimony to our argument that Mr. Adamson must certainly be given the benefit of the doubt as to his remorse and his ability to be rehabilitated.

Judge Ne'elam: Rabbi Finkelman, you may now step down from the witness stand.

(Rabbi Finkelman steps down from the witness stand.)

Commentary on Rabbi Finkelman's Testimony

Rabbi Finkelman's testimony reminds us to read great stories, and each other, with open, compassionate minds attuned to literary ambiguity and moral complexity. However, it leaves us incapable of determining exactly how to deal with Cain as a criminal. How can we be sure what Cain thinks of his actions or if he gives them any real thought at all?

Ultimately, Rabbi Finkelman may be telling us that Cain's motivations — real human motivations — cannot always be subjected to simple judgments and analyses. When all is said and done, Cain must accept the consequences of his behavior once he has been found guilty of his crime. This is the imperative of justice. Yet we can also try to understand Cain, and perhaps even give him the opportunity to act on his remorse and start his life again, once he has paid his societal debt. This is the imperative of mercy.

Justice and mercy: These are the twin foundations of Cain's long story.

Commentary: Wrapping Up Day One of the Trial

As this first day of the trial comes to a close, some of us in the jury may be more confused than we were before we entered the courtroom this morning. At the outset, we might have deluded ourselves with the comfort of knowing that God had obtained a confession from Cain, however oblique it was, after finding Cain standing over Abel's bloodied body. Cain's guilt was never truly in doubt, we might have reasoned, so how hard could his sentencing be?

The answer may simply be: harder than we thought. Evaluating Cain's long story with any sense of clarity is an uphill challenge at best.

The expert witnesses cannot agree about Cain's state of mind before and at the time of the murder. Did Cain take Abel's life in the hot, passionate throes of enraged jealousy? A number of our experts say yes. Did Cain take Abel's life with calculating coldness, after being rejected as God's favorite? A number of our experts say yes. Is Cain a pathetic, broken victim of circumstance who displaced his rage at his darkly enigmatic human and divine fathers onto his hapless brother? A number of our other experts also say yes. Was Cain driven to murder Abel because he lost all faith that life was meaningful and fair, and thus tried to destroy humanity, starting with one quarter of the known population of his world? Still others say yes. Did Cain confess his crime with deep contrition, cynically disavow responsibility for Abel, or whine childishly about the circumstances of his impending punishment, oblivious to the responsibility he bore for it? Rabbi Finkelman says yes to all three, depending on how we read Cain's very few words in response to God.

Meanwhile, God seems too consumed by divine parental love to give us unequivocal deposition testimony about Cain. Cain refuses to speak on his own behalf (perhaps to avoid the risk of incriminating himself in the courtroom, or for some other reason). Exacerbating the confusion is that, as we have seen, in some respects Cain is merely "Exhibit A" in a larger courtroom drama: God's argument with the angels, and their arguments with each other, about whether God should have created humanity at all. If a Cain could just as easily be among humanity's descendants as an Abel, why take the risk of bringing them into the world?

To sentence Cain requires that we the jury, in effect, judge the worthiness of his existence and, by extension, our own. We could say that resolving this argument is irrelevant; after all, God already decided it for us by creating humanity despite the angels' qualms. However, this reasoning ignores the fact that for many of us who yearn for God, God does not appear to be ever present for us. God is not ever offering us that hoped-for reassurance and solace that we matter and that our species can always save itself from the wreckage of our worst excesses. All we have is the cryptic text of the Torah—our "crime report"—beckoning to our ancestors, us, and our descendants to read it, explain it, and live and hope by it.

Tomorrow, the Prosecution will call Sin to the witness stand. God had warned Cain about the seductive powers of this shady gangster from the soul's underworld who detects anger, depression, narcissism, pride, and other human vulnerabilities, then latches on to us. This seducer stands not only behind Cain but behind each of the long stories of our human failings, laughing viciously.

Day Two of the Trial

On day two of the trial, the court will be calling one witness: Sin. We now proceed with Sin's testimony.

First (and Only) Witness of the Day: Sin

Clerk: All rise. The Celestial Court is now in session. Judge Ne'elam presiding. Please be seated.

Judge Ne'elam: Good morning, ladies and gentlemen. Calling this second day of the case of *Cain v. Abel*. Are both sides ready?
Truth: Ready for the People, Your Honor.
Lovingkindness: Ready for the Defense, Your Honor.

Judge Ne'elam: The Defense will call its first witness to testify.
Lovingkindness: Your Honor, we call Sin to the witness stand.
Clerk: Sin, please rise and approach the witness stand.

(Sin approaches the clerk of the court.)

Clerk *(to Sin)*: Do you affirm that you will tell the truth, the whole truth, and nothing but the truth?
Sin: I do.
Clerk: Please be seated.

(Sin is seated. Lovingkindness begins the questioning.)

Lovingkindness: Would you state your full name for the court?

Sin: My formal name is Sin.

Lovingkindness: How did you receive your name?

Sin: My name was not originally Sin. My given name is Ḥata'at, which could be translated as "Sin." The Hebrew is rather ambiguous. Other translations might be "wrongdoing," "purification from ritual pollution," even "missing the bull's eye" in terms of one's behavior. At a certain point I changed Ḥata'at to Sin because no one could pronounce the Hebrew letter *ḥet*. Pronouncing guttural sounds is not easy.

Lovingkindness: I understand you use certain aliases unofficially in other contexts. Would you please tell the court what these are?

Sin: People also refer to me as "Door Coucher," "Crouching Demon," and "Yetzer Ha-Ra."

Lovingkindness: Can you explain how you received these names?

Sin: I got the first two because I look and act like a *rabitzu* demon, one of the monsters of ancient legend who would couch or crouch at the door of your house or some other building. The common belief was that *rabitzu* would pounce on you if you got too close. I too stand alongside people's paths as they go about their daily lives. When they experience a surge of emotion, usually accompanied by strong impulses, I pounce on them. *Yetzer ha-ra*, meaning "the evil impulse," is a technical term Jewish tradition uses to refer to these same impulse surges, whenever they threaten to get out of hand. You might think of me as the manipulator of impulses.

Lovingkindness: Do your aliases reflect your level of influence over people's actions?

Sin: Human beings think so. And I would agree that I have a high degree of influence over human behavior.

Lovingkindness: Does universal human experience corroborate that you are extremely difficult to subdue and channel?

Sin: That is correct.

Lovingkindness: How would you describe your influence over people?

Sin: As I said, I manipulate them when they are emotionally vulnerable, more prone to act on impulse, and to do whatever they might later regret or rationalize. I *am* extremely difficult to subdue, but the fortunate person who does subdue me can channel his or her lust, ambition, ego, anger, self-righteousness, or fear into productive endeavors. It is like harnessing a huge pool of potentially dangerous electricity into a battery.

Lovingkindness: I would like to read to you and the court God's warning to Cain Adamson, the defendant:

"Why are you distressed,
And why is your face fallen?
Surely, if you do right
There is uplift.
But if you do not do right
Sin couches at the door;
Its urge is toward you,
Yet you can be its master." (Gen. 4:6–7)

Is this warning referring specifically to you?

Sin: Yes, it is.

Lovingkindness: Was the language of the warning sufficiently clear for Cain to comprehend that his emotional state or impulses might lead to criminal behavior?

(The Prosecution rises.)

Truth: Objection. Your Honor, the witness is not an expert in reading legal warnings.

Judge Ne'elam: Counsel, reframe the question.

Lovingkindness: Yes, Your Honor. Sin, you identified yourself as the subject of God's warning in the crime report. When you heard God warning Cain, did you think that it was sufficiently clear that he would understand he must not murder Abel?

Sin: Admittedly, even I, the subject of the warning, found it a bit ambiguous. Still . . . yes, Cain should have been able to infer what not to do.

Lovingkindness: Were you present when Cain expressed outrage over God's having rejected his sacrificial offering?

Sin: Present? You are looking at the match that lit the outrage.

Lovingkindness: Did God accurately depict Cain's facial and body language?

Sin: Yes. Cain was so profoundly enraged and depressed, his face literally drooped. I remember thinking, *He's overreacting.* Just because God ignored Cain's sacrifice didn't mean God was rejecting Cain. In fact, God went on to speak with Cain numerous times after the sacrificial offering debacle. God never even spoke to Abel before he died.

Lovingkindness: Did you ever explain this to Cain?

Sin: That is not my job. I am an agent provocateur: I incite people to commit crimes. Besides, I didn't need to explain this. God did.

Lovingkindness: Were you present when God warned Cain?

Sin: Of course. God spoke about me in the third person, but I was there. I am always around, inciting human beings whenever their darkest emotions and impulses are in full throttle. Given my experience and aptitude in the matter, I knew God was wrong.

Lovingkindness: How do you believe God was wrong?

Sin: God insisted that reasoning and forewarning would make Cain retain his self-control around Abel. I knew better. Maybe an angel like you could resist that urge to strike out in anger. But people are not angels. They listen to God, they listen to parents, judges, teachers, friends, therapists, police, clergy . . . Then they usually do whatever I tell them anyway.

Lovingkindness: Did God create you?
Sin: I am 100 percent God's creation.

Lovingkindness: Are you employed by God?
Sin: Yes, but I also work as an independent contractor.

Lovingkindness: Why would God give you the power to tempt people to engage in criminal behavior, while also imploring people not to listen to you, then punishing them for succumbing to your control?
Sin: That is a paradox I cannot answer. You will need to ask God. I just do my job, but I do it so effectively, even God has great difficulty reining me in.

Lovingkindness: You said before that you are like a *rabitzu* demon who pounces on people. I assume this means that you attack people, thus stirring up their aggressions. Did you incite Cain's aggressions so that he would murder his brother?
Sin: In a manner of speaking, I did.

Judge Ne'elam (*pointing toward Lovingkindness*): Counsel, the witness must answer the questions clearly. "In a manner of speaking" is too vague a response for this court.
Lovingkindness: Yes, Your Honor. Sin, did you seduce Cain into killing Abel?
Sin: I urged him on, but his actions were his own doing.

Lovingkindness: Did you stir up his aggressions? Did Cain murder Abel under your influence?
Sin: Yes, he was very much under my influence.

Lovingkindness: Please explain to the court how you influenced Cain.
Sin: God warned Cain to restrain himself, but I convinced Cain that Abel was the ultimate cause of his pain. I reassured Cain that his suffering would cease once he rid himself of Abel.

Lovingkindness: So, you got Cain to view his brother as the perpetrator of his pain, and to view himself as the victim, correct? In short, you convinced Cain to kill Abel by convincing him to scapegoat his brother.

Sin: Scapegoating is a strong word, but yes, I convinced him.

Lovingkindness: Did Cain recognize that he was scapegoating his brother?

Sin: In my experience, no one who scapegoats someone else is ever able to recognize or admit it.

Lovingkindness: How would you reconcile your testimony with that of yesterday's expert witnesses, who offered this court a variety of probable motivations for the defendant's actions, but never mentioned you manipulating Cain in this way?

Sin: Those expert witnesses correctly asserted that Cain viewed himself as superior to Abel as well as a hapless recipient of his father's mistreatment. However, they missed one important clue in God's warning to Cain that reveals just how powerful an effect I had on Cain. Cain was feeling very self-pitying when God found him licking his wounded pride and warned him about his rage. I knew that whatever God said to him, Cain would likely only hear the last few words and play them obsessively over and over in his head. Sure enough, Cain was kicking in the entrance of Abel's sheep pen, mumbling on and on about me — "You can be its master . . ." — when he literally met me crouching at the door.

Lovingkindness: What happened then?

Sin: Cain was so shocked and disgusted by the sight of me, he started kicking me. Recall that God asked him explicitly about his being enraged and about his body drooping to the ground in utter depression. What better way to escape his own smallness and weakness than to beat on me? But I knew how to play that boy. Immediately I stood up and pounced on him. As he continued to mumble, "You can be *its* master," I kept echoing the same words, sadly, empathetically. Soon, Cain was weeping in my arms. I cooed to him, "Poor Cain. That little shit, Abel, is nothing more than an *it*, not even a person, a mere exhalation, *hevel*, vapor. *It* took from you what was rightfully yours. *It* took from us what was ours. Can we master *Abel*, that *it*? Of course we can, and we damn well should." How I loved twisting God's words totally out of context, amplifying their echo in Cain's head, and enticing him into displacing his self-pitying rage onto his "It" of a brother.

Lovingkindness: Why did you do this to him?

Sin: This is what I do for a living. As I said before, I like to do my job well.

Lovingkindness: No further questions for this witness, Your Honor.

Judge Ne'elam: Does prosecuting counsel move to cross-examine?

Truth *(rising)*: Thank You, Your Honor. Sin, do you acknowledge that God warned Cain about the potential impact of his emotions on his future actions?

Sin: Yes, but he never mentioned *Abel* explicitly.

Truth: Do you acknowledge that God was clear with Cain, both that he needed to stay away from you and that he could control you, howbeit with great difficulty?

Sin: Yes, God said those things; God believes those are true. But honestly, God is pathetic and ineffective. I am desire, rage, the demon angel who slept with Cain's mother. I am the cancer that ate the raw flesh in Cain's twisted heart while he pounded the rock into Abel's head.

Truth: Do you acknowledge that, however difficult God's warning to Cain about you might have been to follow, the fact that God even warned him only makes sense if Cain was free to listen to, or to reject, that warning? As such, wasn't Cain at least theoretically free to choose to control his rage and not murder his brother?

Sin: When it comes to contending with me, freedom to choose is largely an illusion. I am very difficult to subdue. I am an extremely formidable force.

Truth: Answer my question, please. Would you agree that, with your aggressive and alluring manipulations fully recognized by this court, in principle, however infinitesimal the odds, Cain *might* have been able to bring you under control? For example, couldn't Cain have wrestled you to the ground before you pounced on him and seduced him?

Sin: Theoretically, I guess he could have. As I said before, the lucky person who does subdue me can channel his most powerful impulses into very productive things . . .

Truth: No further questions for the witness, Your Honor.

Judge Ne'elam: Sin, you may now step down from the witness stand.

(Sin steps down from the witness stand.)

Commentary on Sin's Testimony

Everyone in the courtroom could not help but stare at the ugly — yet bizarrely alluring — misshapen creature wound up and ready to pounce. Sin, a monster grafted onto a voluptuous woman, seemed to be neither man nor woman, but both, projecting maleness *and* femaleness. The creature also appeared at once utterly foreign and terrifying, and yet so intimate . . . like we knew Sin, like we are Sin too.

Yesterday, Truth made the case that God's laconic warning to Cain in Genesis 4:7 ("Sin couches at the door; / Its urge is toward you, / Yet you can be its master") was clear enough for Cain to have known he had to control his will to do evil; still, Cain chose to ignore God's warning. Countering this argument, Lovingkindness maintained that Cain deserved clemency because murder had not yet occurred in the world, and thus Cain could not have stood forewarned about an entirely unprecedented human experience.

Today, Lovingkindness brought Sin to the witness stand to prove that Cain did not have total control over his actions. Cain was duped and doomed by Sin's belligerent and seductive power. That force was so overwhelming, Cain did not have it within him to bring Sin under control. What is more, Cain couldn't even imagine or prepare for the potency of Sin's influence on him, because God's description of Sin's power had been too vague. Indeed, commentators and translators consider Genesis 4:7 to be one of the most difficult, ambiguous passages in the entire Torah.[1] On the basis of these mitigating circumstances, Lovingkindness argued, we the jury should mete out a less severe punishment to Cain. Perhaps we might even be inclined to acquit Cain by reason of temporary insanity, so potent is Sin's ability to distort a person's thinking.[2]

During the cross-examination, the Prosecution pressed to have Sin acknowledge that Cain (or, for that matter, any human being) had the free will to turn away from Sin's powerful allure. Sin's testimony stressed that resistance was nearly, but not entirely, impossible.

Cain's culpability may rest on whether he was truly free not to murder his brother. The Hebrew for God's promise to Cain that he could achieve self-mastery over Sin is the ambiguous phrase "ve-attah timshol bo." It could mean that God is "commanding" Cain to master Sin, that God is "giving" Cain absolute assurance that he will master Sin, or that God is "promising" Cain the possibility of freely mastering Sin.[3] Our standard English translation uses the last option, though we cannot be sure this is what the text really means.

OTHER PREVAILING QUESTIONS

Another prevailing question is why God speaks to Cain using the imagery of Sin. Why doesn't God come right out and warn him directly, "Cain, your anger will impel you to strike your brother and you will kill him; you must be the master of your rage"?

At first glance, it is not clear if God's description of Sin is intended to be taken literally or metaphorically, as a personification of our most base human impulses. The Torah teaches that God works alone in creating and governing the world. Yet, as Sin implied on the witness stand, Sin has a backstory, rooted in popular ancient Near Eastern beliefs, about demonic powers that might challenge even God. Perhaps God is employing graphic and grotesque imagery—"the demon couching/crouching at the door"—to awaken Cain to the dark, toxic brew of sadness, rage, and self-pity bubbling inside him that threatens to tip him over the edge into murder. The Torah might be presenting us with what ancient people believed was a literal demonic and malevolent force that could attack or enter us from the outside, similar to an early Christian portrayal of Satan.[4] Jewish literature, particularly (but not exclusively) its folklore, contains many stories and images of demons and other nonhuman powers, creations of God that cause human beings, and sometimes God, a great deal of trouble.[5]

Most likely, the Torah is presenting Sin metaphorically to describe rebellious human impulses and behavior. This particularly graphic metaphor is fitting because it was a "horror story" image common to biblical audiences. People of that time listening to the Cain and Abel story would have found the couching or crouching demon terrifyingly familiar. This would have been a potent way to convey how powerful and dangerous envy-fueled rage can be.

Even though Sin spoke extensively in the courtroom, this witness's true character remains somewhat of an enigma to us. On the stand, Sin appeared to take the form of two living, symbiotic characters, two parts of a whole to which Cain succumbed: seductiveness and monstrous belligerence. For its part, the crime report described Sin as someone or something seeking to "jump" Cain while he was on his path. Sin was couching or—as some translators suggest—crouching. Ought Sin to be imagined as a seducer, an animal of prey, a monster, all of these, or something else?

God also refers to Sin as if Cain is already familiar with this troubling character. When were the two previously acquainted? Did Cain perhaps learn about sinful impulses from his parents' experience of being seduced by the snake into violating God's instructions?

ORIGINS OF THE IMAGE OF SIN

Other questions emerge from examining the origin of the Sin image. As Sin alluded to during testimony, the biblical Hebrew verb for couching or crouching, *roveitz*, is closely related to the Akkadian word *rabitzu*.[6] *Rabitzu* were court officials who had the unenviable task of forcing defendants to show up at court or pay court-ordered fines. *Rabitzu* were so detested by the citizenry that the term was later "demonized"[7]—that is, applied as a description of demons and evil spirits. *Rabitzu* were believed to crouch like animals near the doorways of houses, temples, and places of business. They waited to pounce on unsuspecting outsiders, but they also protected occupants of these buildings—insiders. Later biblical Hebrew borrowed the noun *rabitzu* and turned it into a verb, *roveitz*, meaning "couch" or "crouch." God's warning to Cain implies both meanings. Sin is a despised, feared, and litigious demon who couches or crouches at Cain's "door" with "official court sanction" (that is, God). Sin is at the ready to cross Cain's path or burrow through the door of Cain's heart.[8] Sin will pounce on Cain with ostensibly unstoppable force, supposedly to drag him before a judge, but more likely to drag him down into hell.[9]

Though it uses mythological imagery, the Torah refuses to hand absolute spiritual or moral power to Sin. The biblical description of Sin in Genesis 4:7 does not dwell on demonic forces but emphasizes the excruciating challenge to human freedom of doing what is morally right when we are confronted with this formidable opponent. Nonetheless, God provides Cain with the power to heed warnings, choose moral behavior, and control the *rabitzu* within. We humans do possess the God-given freedom to "rise up and wrestle Sin to the ground," to defang the *rabitzu* as it were, through our exercise of self-control.

SIN — A TROUBLING TEMPTRESS?

Disturbing questions concerning Sin and gender also emerge from our encounter with God's warning. Earlier in the Bible, in Genesis 3:16, Eve is punished for her particular role in the Tree of Knowledge incident. Henceforth, her sexual urges will be for her husband, who will subjugate her sexually and physically: "And to the woman God said, 'Your urge [*te-shu-ka-tekh*] shall be for your husband, and he shall rule over you [*Ve-hu yimshol bakh*].'"

For modern readers, God's statement is deeply troubling, especially given earlier biblical statements that point toward equality between men and women, both created in God's image.[10] In this light, Genesis 3:16 may come across as a rigidly sexist rationalization of men's sexual and physical subjugation of women. Even more troubling, the idea of blaming women for Sin is echoed metaphorically in God's warning to Cain. Genesis 4:7 tells us, "God said to Cain, . . . 'Sin's urge [*te-shu-ka-to*] shall be for you, / But you may be sin's master [*Ve-attah timshol bo*].'" Sin is being compared to an erotically seductive woman who might lure Cain into losing control and engaging in horribly destructive behavior unless he, like his father who rules over his mother, exercises control over Sin the seductress.

Yet the matter is not that simple. In truth, the Hebrew text *la-petaḥ ḥata'at roveitz*, meaning "Sin couches/is a crouching demon at the door,"[11] casts Sin as a mix of male and female, a hypermasculine creature-monster *and* an attractively seductive woman."[12] Since Hebrew is a gendered language, its different words assuming either female or male forms, a Hebrew noun and verb are supposed to have gender agreement. However, the combination of *ḥata'at* with *roveitz* violates this basic Hebrew rule. While *ḥata'at* (Sin) is a female noun form, *roveitz* (couch/crouch) is a male verb form. This strange feature of the story has puzzled Bible teachers and scholars for centuries.[13]

Perhaps the Torah is consciously employing the grammatical mismatch to teach us that Sin, the "male" monster *and* the "female" temptress, is "gender-fluid."[14] Cain, the first human being to usurp God's rule over humanity through murder, was a man, but Sin cannot be neatly "gendered" or otherwise categorized, just as human impulses and choices cannot be easily ordered or predicted. Sin can pounce on and/or seduce any of us in many different ways.

Meanwhile, a further comparison of God's warnings to Eve and Cain reveals a subtle, significant shift of emphasis in God's plea to Cain. Adam *will* rule over Eve and her desires, men *must* rule over women and their desires, but (as we saw above) Cain *can* rule over Sin.

THE *YETZER HA-RA* IN RABBINIC TRADITION

Yet why did God allow Sin to crouch at our doors in the first place? Wouldn't it have been easier and safer for us had God created Cain without the capacity to succumb to the envy and rage that incited him to kill? How much anguish could humanity have been spared had God simply denied us the seductive and belligerent chokehold of Sin from the very beginning, even if it meant losing some or all of our moral freedom? As it is, Sin makes the free exercise of good moral judgment and impulse control so difficult, it sometimes feels like a futile battle. How could—or why would—a just God inflict on us such injustice and unjust suffering?

Our expert witnesses, the Rabbis of the Talmud, were disturbed by these questions about God's relationship with humanity. As we heard in Sin's testimony, the Rabbis referred to Sin as *yetzer ha-ra*, roughly translated as "the evil nature."[15]

The Rabbis held different beliefs about human evil and divine justice (as well as much else). One Rabbinic view about *yetzer ha-ra* appears in the very unsettling *mashal* story that follows.[16]

Torah can be compared to a life-giving medical treatment.

This can be explained by the parable of a man who struck his son with a violent blow, then placed a bandage on his wound.

He said to his son, "My son, as long as this bandage is on your wound, eat what you like, drink what you like, bathe in hot or cold water, and you have no reason to be fearful (that the wound will worsen). But, if you remove the bandage, rest assured, the wound will become a corrosive ulcer."

In like fashion, God said to the Jewish people, "My children, I created *yetzer ha-ra*, yet I also created Torah as its cure. If you busy yourselves with Torah, you will not be delivered into the power of *yetzer ha-ra*."

As is it is written, "Surely, if you do right (by following Torah), there is uplift."

God then said to them, "But if you do not busy yourselves with Torah, you will be delivered into the power of *yetzer ha-ra*."

As it is also written, "Sin couches at the door (of your heart)."

God further said to them, "Moreover, all of *yetzer ha-ra*'s business is focused on (enslaving) you."

As it is written, "Its urge is toward you."

God finally said to them, "And if you choose, you may rule over it (through Torah)."

As it is also written, "Yet you can master it."[17]

In this story, the father is God, the son is the Jewish people and, by implication, all human beings. Just as the man strikes his son and then offers him medical intervention and advice, God "strikes" human beings by creating within us *yetzer ha-ra*, and then creates Torah to protect us from its most damaging effects.

What does this unsettling comparison mean at a deeper level? Striking your child to the point of inflicting a dangerous wound is morally repugnant and, in our society, a crime. Today we rightly condemn such behavior as child abuse. Does this analogy imply that God's "wounding" us with *yetzer ha-ra* is an inexplicable act of abusive violence against humanity?

Other reasons might account for the father's violence. Perhaps he is defending himself against his son's unmentioned aggressiveness.

Possibly his blow was a tragic accident. Also, acceptable standards for discipline of children in ancient societies were different than our own. But any attempt to rationalize or soften the harshness of this *mashal* only underscores its dark and suggestive ambiguity. The storyteller seems to have purposely excluded any rationale for the father's hitting his son with such violence, and, in any event, no justification for his actions would change the reality that he severely wounded his child.

Moving from the story to its discordant *nimshal* (the application of the parable), we encounter God the Parent inflicting the wound of *yetzer ha-ra* on us with no disclosure about God's motivations for doing so. Could this *mashal* be read as a human protest against God in which we bitterly complain: "How can we be just when *yetzer ha-ra* oppresses us so harshly? Why would You, our God and Parent who demands that we behave justly, do this to us?"[18]

Note that the *mashal* is not arguing for the Christian concept of original sin, a spiritual stain to be washed out of us by God's grace alone.[19] However, it does hold that our impulsive drive to do terribly bad things is an indelible part of human nature. The Torah accepts human darkness and weakness as givens—which is why God never explains Sin's existence to Cain but only tells Cain that Sin is a nasty fact of life with no further explanation. The philosopher Leon Kass asserts that the story of Cain and Abel is, in part, about how "there are no natural impulses or passions that seek to unite brother with brother."[20] He is suggesting that the Torah sees rivalry, Sin's handmaiden, not love, as the natural condition of families—a terrifying perspective.

However, the end of the *nimshal* offers us a measure of hope. Just as the bandage over the son's wound keeps him alive and functioning for as long as he chooses to wear it, freely choosing to learn and follow the Torah allows us to rein in and control the damaging effects of Sin/*yetzer ha-ra*. Significantly, the child's wound can never be cured, but the bandage can keep him sufficiently healthy. So too, even Torah cannot cure us of our worst urges to sin, but Torah is God's most powerful means of helping us to struggle with and master the ever-present impulses within us.

The teaching concludes with a brilliant new insight into God's warning to Cain in Genesis 4:7.[21] God, we have learned, was rather vague when exhorting Cain to master Sin/*yetzer ha-ra*. Imagine Cain arguing with God in his own preemptive self-defense, "You created this monster. You admonished me with a nebulous warning about how I could control Sin without ever giving me the tools to succeed at the task. So, when I was drowning in my own feelings of rage, rejection, and depression and the seductive beast came charging toward me, what did You expect would happen?"

Obviously, since he lived well before the revelation of Torah, Cain would not have had this master tool for self-discipline lauded by the *nimshal*. He would not have had access to Torah values, ethics, and prohibitions. He could not have engaged in Torah study to further self-control, responsibility, compassion, and justice. The Rabbis were not necessarily suggesting that God literally offered him Torah.

They were making a different point: Succumbing to evil temptations is not a fait accompli. God has helped us humans to cultivate other emotions, qualities, and social tools, among them compassion, familial responsibility, and law, to effectively counter Sin. Further, *yetzer ha-tov*, the inclination toward good behavior described in talmudic writing, might not be as powerful or indelible as *yetzer ha-ra*, but it is equally real.[22] The Torah is the finest Jewish expression of all these tools and capacities.

As part of this, the Torah spells out a vision of society based on covenantal relationships with God and others that we can choose. It refuses to hand a victory to human beings' fratricidal impulses. As Kass writes about later sibling stories of Genesis that echo and respond to Cain and Abel: "The new way [of family and social life] . . . under the covenant . . . requires, at the very least, not destroying your brother."[23]

How do we internalize this vision so we can live by it? The Torah's demands are held forth by our *mashal* story as Cain's path to goodness, even if they cannot easily penetrate a heart so broken by jeal-ous rage and determined to wreak vengeful havoc. God the universal Parent gifted to Cain the Torah as the means to self-reflection, repen-tance, and self-correction. The antidote could preserve Cain's life, even if it could not cure his worst disease. Thus, God offered Cain a much stronger defense against Sin than we had first thought when we read the crime report.

Sin slinks out the courtroom door, too quickly to be stopped for an interview. Now, after day two of the trial, we know considerably more about this intoxicating creature. For one, we know that Sin manipulates us into victimizing others by deceiving us into believ-ing that we are the real victims. But are we any wiser about how to master Sin when Sin jumps us at each door we pass?

At the very end of the day, Sin finally admitted to this court that, at least theoretically, Cain could have controlled Sin by wrestling him/her to the ground before Sin pounced on him and seduced him. If Cain's sentence rests entirely on whether he was truly free not to murder his brother, we may at least be wiser about Cain's culpability.

His claim to our understanding and forgiveness also rests on a different matter: his family history. Tomorrow, we will hear the tes-timony of his parents, Eve and Adam.

Day Three of the Trial

On day three of the trial, the court will call the following witnesses: (1) Eve, mother of Cain; (2) Adam, father of Cain. We begin with the testimony of the witness Eve.

First Witness of the Day: Eve

Clerk: All rise. The Celestial Court is now in session. Judge Ne'elam presiding. Please be seated.

Judge Ne'elam: Good morning, ladies and gentlemen. Calling this third day of the case of *Cain v. Abel*. Are both sides ready?

Truth: Ready for the People, Your Honor.

Lovingkindness: Ready for the Defense, Your Honor.

Judge Ne'elam: The Prosecution will call the first witness to testify.

Truth: Your Honor, we call Eve to the witness stand.

Clerk: Eve, please rise and approach the witness stand.

(Eve approaches the clerk of the court.)

Clerk *(to Eve)*: Do you affirm that you will tell the truth, the whole truth, and nothing but the truth?

Eve: I do.

Clerk: Please be seated.

(Eve is seated. Truth begins the questioning.)

Truth: Would you state your full name for the court?

Eve: My English name is Eve. My original, formal Hebrew name is Ḥavva Eim-Kol Chai, which means "Living one, the mother of all life."

Truth: How did you receive your formal Hebrew name?

Eve: My husband Adam named me this just before our expulsion from Eden.

Truth: Why did he give you this name?

Eve: After we ate from the Tree of Knowledge, we discovered sex and came to believe that the snake had told us the truth. Eating from the tree would not result in our deaths, as God had warned, at least not immediately. We recognized that we could achieve immortality through childbirth. I and all women after me would have that power. Of course, we learned the hard way that this power is chained to our mortality. We could make children, but we would also die.

Truth: The crime report mentions that you named your first child Kayyin, or Cain in English, as a play on the Hebrew verb *kanah*, meaning "to acquire" or "to create." Is that so? Is it fair to say that, just as your husband Adam named you, Ḥavva Eim-Kol Chai, "the mother of all life," you named your first child Kayyin/Cain to signify your power?

Eve: Yes, that is true, but there is more. Kayyin can also mean "to fashion," "to shape," "to give form to something."[1] I was thrilled to have formed this beautiful baby as a partner with God. I loved feeling like God's equal as co-bearer of our child. I was also grateful that Cain looked like his father, Samael.

Truth: Rabbi ben Uzziel previously testified that Samael was Cain's father. Are you now corroborating his testimony?

Eve: Yes, I am. Samael, a divine being, one of God's angels, is Cain's biological father. I remember what a wonderful feeling it was, rocking that precious baby in my arms, knowing he was partly divine.

Truth: It seems you gave Cain considerable parental nourishment and love. Would you agree that he had a better maternal upbringing than your second son, Abel, who, according to the crime report, you didn't even name?

Eve: I did name him. Abel didn't acquire his name from nowhere. But to be honest, I was ashamed to let people know about him.

Truth: Why were you ashamed to tell people about Abel, whom you conceived with your husband, but proud to speak of Cain, whom you conceived with your lover?

Eve: I made a conscious decision to have a relationship with Samael. With Adam, it was very different. One day, long after Cain was born, Adam forced himself on me in a fit of abusive rage. How was I not supposed to feel ambivalent about the boy I conceived that way?

Truth: You did not want Abel?

Eve: I wanted him, and I loved him, but my love was mixed with resentment and anguish. And I tried—desperately—to get Cain to love him.

Truth: In your estimation, then, did you do your best as a parent to raise your sons fairly and well, and also teach them to treat each other properly?

Eve: I believe I did. I was not perfect, sometimes I showed my biases, but I made real efforts to put aside many of my feelings to raise both boys fairly throughout the course of their lives.

Truth: How do you understand your and Adam's exclusion from nearly all of the crime report? Were you, in fact, present in your children's adult lives?

Eve: Of course we were. The exclusion hurts—though I can understand it in terms of influence. As Cain and Abel grew older, it got harder for us to have the influence we wanted on the boys. The relationship between Cain and Abel deteriorated— really, Cain grew more hostile toward Abel. It broke my heart.

Truth: Were you worried that Cain might act on his hostility? Did you ever warn him about controlling his aggressive impulses?

Eve: Yes, I was very worried, and I tried to warn him.

Truth: Please explain to the jury what you mean when you say you tried to warn him. We have no record of you—or Adam—having said anything to Cain.

Eve: Adam and I have been very disconnected since our eviction from Eden. During Adam's frequent absences, I took it on myself to explain to Cain how powerful—and dangerous—acting on impulse can be.

Truth: How did you communicate this to Cain?

Eve: I explained to him what had happened when I ate from the Tree of Knowledge, how it led to Adam and me being banished from Eden.

Truth: How did Cain respond?

Eve: He didn't say much. Cain never spoke to me about his feelings.

Truth: We heard testimony from Sin yesterday. Had you met Sin before yesterday?

Eve: No. I had heard about Sin. I suspect that when the snake lured and framed me in Eden, he was subcontracted by Sin to work on me.

Truth: As you know, Cain was associating himself with Sin. Did Cain give you any indication that he understood the danger of associating with Sin?

Eve: Cain never spoke to me about his friends or associates.

Truth: The forensic assessment analyzed God's expulsion order to you and Adam alongside God's crime report about Cain and found them to be startlingly close in language. Weren't they, in fact, so close that Cain, knowing your family history, should have understood God's warning to him as a mirror of God's earlier warning to you?[2]

Eve: I suppose. Look, it's very difficult for me to understand what my precious son the murderer did and did not understand.

Truth: Yes or no: Would *you* have understood that warning, in light of your history?

Lovingkindness (*rising*): Objection, Your Honor, Eve is not on trial. What she might have understood is not at issue here. The only relevant question is what Cain himself did understand.

Truth: Your Honor, I am merely trying to establish whether a reasonable person who knew the family background would have understood God's warning to Cain in that context.

Judge Ne'elam: I will allow it. Eve, you may answer the question.

Eve: Yes, I would have understood. But God's warning to me before I ate from the Tree of Knowledge was far more explicit than God's warning to Cain.

Truth: The point is, yes, you would have understood. Eve, I notice bruises on your arms and legs. Where did you get them?

Eve: I fell . . . over some people.

Truth: Some people, Eve? What people? Adam was off in the fields. The only people around were you, Cain, and maybe Abel, who was dying or dead.

Eve: (no answer)

Truth: Eve, when you are on the witness stand, you need to answer my questions. From where—or whom—did you get those bruises?

Eve: (no answer)

Lovingkindness *(rising)*: Your Honor, honestly, the Prosecution is badgering the witness. It is immaterial, harassment, and cruel.

Truth: Your Honor, the witness is hiding evidence of her involvement in this case. I believe she is trying to cover for the defendant in order to mitigate the severity of his sentencing.

Judge Ne'elam: Counsel, you are badgering the witness, and I have no idea where your examination is going. Unless you can justify your line of questioning, you must desist.

(Truth motions to co-counsel, Peace, who provides a file containing one document.)

Truth: Your Honor, we just now have in our possession a note written by Eve indicating that she was far more involved in her interventions with Cain than she has admitted under oath. In fact, the note indicates that she attempted to physically intervene, howbeit too late, to prevent Cain from murdering Abel, which is how she sustained these bruises. We ask that this note, which I now hold in my hand, be entered into the court record.

(Truth holds up the letter so both the Judge and Eve can see it.)

Judge Ne'elam *(to Eve)*: Did you write this note?

Eve: Well . . . yes.

Lovingkindness *(rising)*: Objection, Your Honor! The Defense was given no prior warning regarding the existence of such a note.

Truth: Your Honor, that couldn't be helped. This is a recent but extremely pertinent development.

Judge Ne'elam: Since Eve has confirmed she wrote this note, it is material evidence. I have to allow it.

Truth *(handing Eve the note)*: Eve, would you please read to the court what you wrote?

Eve: Why? What possible good could come of making me relive this? I was in way too much pain at that point to have written anything rational . . .

Truth: I am sorry, Eve, but this is a necessary part of our proceeding. Please read your note, which I understand the poet Dan Pagis went on later to transcribe and title "Written in Pencil in the Sealed Railway Car."

Eve:

> here in this carload
> i am eve
> with abel my son
> if you see my other son
> cain son of man
> tell him i[3]

Lovingkindness *(rising)*: Your Honor, this is all very confusing and completely irrelevant to this case. Opposing counsel has advanced the note as offering proof of the witness's bodily intervention during her children's violent quarrel. While it is true that the witness appears to associate it with a traumatic memory, I ask you, where in this note is there even a speck of evidence that Eve sustained bruises when trying to prevent Cain from murdering Abel? This note must be struck from the official record. It is far more obtuse than God's warning to Cain.

Truth: Your Honor, the witness affirmed that she authored the note, in which she maintained that she wrote it while forced brutally into a boxcar. We have every reason to assume that she was being transported to her death with Abel, and who knows how many other innocent people bound for slaughter at the hands of Cain. I logically deduce her failed intervention from the fact that she wound up being thrown into that death-car along with Abel and all the other victims, past, present, and future. As she was pressed down under the bodies of the soon-to-be-murdered, she felt she desperately needed to reach out to her son.

Judge Ne'elam: Counsel, enough. I'll allow the note as material evidence, but your "logical deduction" sounds like speculation to me. Does Defense counsel want to cross-examine the witness?

Lovingkindness: Yes, Your Honor.

Judge Ne'elam: Counsel, you may proceed.

Lovingkindness *(rising again)*: Thank You, Your Honor. Eve, earlier you testified that you always felt closer to Cain than to Abel, even though you tried to express your love for them equally, correct?

Eve: Yes. I tried to treat them fairly and equitably, but I realize I sent a lot of ambiguous messages.

Lovingkindness: Would it be fair to say that sometimes Cain experienced your love for him as if it were his alone, and other times he saw your love expressly directed toward his brother?

Eve: Yes, as I said, in retrospect I sent a lot of mixed messages.

Lovingkindness: And you testified earlier that Adam was frequently absent from the family.

Eve: Yes, Adam and I had largely gone our separate ways.

Lovingkindness: What was Cain's relationship like with his step-father?

Eve: They had a horrible relationship. Cain was always trying to impress Adam, and Adam never gave him what he wanted. Adam was always distant toward him. I couldn't do anything about it. When Cain was finally old enough to hear the truth, I told him that Samael, not Adam, was his father. Their relationship never improved, yet telling Cain the truth did seem to help him understand why Adam treated him as he did.

Lovingkindness: So, from both you and from Adam, Cain would not have experienced what we would call consistently loving parenting, is that correct?

Eve: Yes.

Lovingkindness: What effect do you think this had on Cain?

Eve: I don't know. . . . I have often asked myself that very question. I worry that the lack of consistency, frankly the barely veiled hostility from Adam, along with having been abandoned by Samael, may have contributed to Cain's rage, which precipitated Abel's death.

Lovingkindness: Thank you. Eve, the Prosecution has made an unverified claim that you wrote a factual note of your experience after you attempted unsuccessfully to prevent Cain from murdering Abel. You protested that you were in no shape to have written anything rational, given the intense pain you were experiencing in those moments. Is it possible that nothing you wrote in this note transcribed by Mr. Pagis actually happened? Did you possibly write it as a way of dealing with the immediate trauma of the murder?

Eve: It's possible. I don't know. As I said, I was in no state of mind to think rationally at that moment . . . (*becoming further animated*). But one thing I was right about—it *was* a boxcar, every inch and breath and movement of our family's life *was* a stench-filled cattle car that squeezed the life from Cain . . . squeezed the life from us all.

Lovingkindness: No further questions for this witness, Your Honor.

Judge Ne'elam: Eve, you may step down from the witness stand.

(Eve steps down from the witness stand.)

Commentary on Eve's Testimony

When the Israeli poet Dan Pagis was fourteen, he escaped from a Nazi concentration camp in the Ukraine. Eventually, by 1946, he had made his way to Palestine.[4]

Today, Yad Vashem, the International Holocaust Authority and Museum in Jerusalem, displays Pagis's poem "Written in Pencil in the Sealed Railway Car" right above the Nazi-era boxcar on permanent exhibit. Visitors can barely imagine—if at all—the experience he packs into his tight poem: Mother Eve's agony scrawled in her last words on the wall of that railway car, as she and her victim child, Abel, along with all her descendants, suffocate slowly, like penned cattle, on their way to the death camps.

And yet, imagination is precisely what Pagis demands of the reader to confront the enormous evil of the Holocaust and of all genocide. Up to this point everything we know about Cain and Abel's parents suggests a mother and father divided against each other, in good part over their children. Eve's testimony implies a far more complex, involved relationship; Pagis suggestively develops its agonizing implications for humanity. In the boxcar, Eve, symbolic mother of all humanity, is bonded with Abel, symbolic ancestor of every victim of inhumanity. Like her silent younger son, Eve too is dying brutally at the hands of her beloved son Cain, the murdering child presumably hiding and unaccounted for.

In Pagis's retelling of the story, Eve, absent from the crime report's account, is now tragically and fully present. Pagis challenges us to think about Eve longing for Cain while also indicting him for brutalizing his brother. She also has a voice, especially at the end of Abel's life. Pagis transforms her into an active participant in both her sons' lives, though in a bitterly ironic way, as she rides toward a violent death.

Presented as Eve's damning note, Pagis's poem is a modern midrash, a means for us the jury to explore the universal implications of Cain and Abel's fatal conflict through the particular lens of the Holocaust. Whenever and wherever one person victimizes another, Eve and her victimized children—progenitors of all human beings—can be found, dying together in that boxcar. Hebrew literature scholar Anne Lerner explains that by reworking the story of Eve and her sons in this way, Pagis "implies that from its conception, the human project carried the seeds of inhumanity."[5] Eve suffocates with Abel in a tragic solidarity of victimization, while searching to the very end for her beloved Cain, the murderer of her family: "if you see my elder son / cain son of man / tell him i." Tell him that I . . . what? All sense, logic, and hope dissolve into the choking air surrounding Eve's brutally amputated statement. Eve's cry against Cain, along with her desperate search for him as she waits to die with Abel, is so loud, it cannot be ignored, precisely because it is the cry of the mother of both the victim *and* the murderer. With Pagis's pen, Eve, "the mother of all life," is transformed into the eternally suffering "mother of all death."

A more nuanced image of Eve is not exclusively an invention of Pagis's poetic imagination. A *peshat* (simple, contextual) reading of Eve's story in Genesis portrays her as a complex, paradigmatic character who should not be reduced to a sinful temptress bringing fatal trouble to the world, as many early midrashic sources do.[6] She is a far-from-perfect, yet bold, proactive family leader whose actions bring trouble *and* badly needed change, death, *and* life.[7]

Looking at mother and child, readers might infer that Cain is merely perpetuating Eve's relentless dialectic of death and life, transgression and progress. However, a subtle yet critical distinction exists between Eve and Cain, one she alludes to in her testimony about her name, Ḥavva, the mother of all life. Eve's name—her very substance—breathes the possibility, even the imperative, of new life for all human beings, *without distinction between one person and another.*

After fratricide, repentance, and, later, exile East of Eden, Cain too will exercise the power of naming and bringing forth new life, but his future choices will reveal a distortion of Eve's and Adam's naming and life-giving powers: "Cain knew his wife, and she conceived and bore Enoch. And he (Cain) then founded a city and named the city after his son Enoch" (Gen. 4:17). Our expert witness Nachmanides understands Cain's building project as a pathetic quest for survival and continuity after murder and exile. Because he is condemned by God to wander, Cain decides to build a city for his son, Enoch, and to name it explicitly after him. That way, at least Enoch can settle in peace and safety despite the curse of exile God imposed on his father. Yet Cain's effort will prove to be pure futility. He will wander the rest of his life back and forth between homelessness and the city he will never finish building.[8] Is this because, unlike his mother's mission to be the mother of all life, Cain's mission is to preserve only the lives of those he loves? If so, it is this distortion of the mission to preserve life that condemns Cain the builder to perpetual exile: Can he hope to civilize human existence when he cannot civilize himself?

From Eve's testimony, we can surmise that Eve may see all of this at one time and see none of it at another. Like God during the deposition, Eve seems to be too blinded by the parental desire to protect both of her children, the victim and the murderer, to make a sober judgment of Cain's culpability. This witness's honesty is corrupted not by cowardice but by love.

Thus, another part/persona/role of Cain appears to be the suffering "demon" child loved by God and mother. Does the Cain we see reflected in his mother's eyes provide a mitigating circumstance by which we are to judge Cain in this courtroom: a kind of love and mercy unmoored from punishment and justice?

Now we must return to the courtroom. The Defense is about to examine the next witness: Adam.

Second Witness of the Day: Adam

Judge Ne'elam: The Defense will call the next witness to testify.
Lovingkindness: Your Honor, we call Adam to the witness stand.

Clerk: Adam, please rise and approach the witness stand.

(Adam approaches the clerk of the court.)

Clerk: Do you affirm that you will tell the truth, the whole truth, and nothing but the truth?
Adam: I do.
Clerk: Please be seated.

(Adam is seated. Lovingkindness begins the questioning.)

Lovingkindness: Would you please state your full name for the court.
Adam: Adam Ha-Rishon.

Lovingkindness: How did you get your name?

Adam: Adam derives from the Hebrew word *adamah*, meaning "earth." I'm what's known as an "earth-person." Adam Ha-Rishon means "First Man." God spawned me first, so I got the paradoxical distinction of a last name that means, literally, "the first one." According to the Rabbis, your expert witnesses, I'm supposed to be the primordial man from whom all of humanity later descends. It's all stupid. I finished last in every aspect of my life, and I was the only one on earth besides my family.

Lovingkindness: What is your profession?

Adam: I'm a farmer. It's a miserable life. My work is demeaning and backbreaking, and most of what I manage to pull from the ground are thorns and thistles. My family and I barely survive. Forget about breaking even; I can't even grow enough produce to feed myself. Chewing on wild grass would be more nourishing.[9] And I have God to thank for it all.

Lovingkindness: Please try to refrain from editorializing when answering my questions. What role has God played in your misfortune?

Adam: I was implicated in a very serious breach by my wife. God forced us out of Eden and condemned me and my descendants to struggle with farming.

Lovingkindness: Implicated? The court's understanding is that you actively participated in that breach, the "Tree of Knowledge incident," correct?

Adam: I was implicated. Had I known the source of the fruit Eve tantalizingly waved before my eyes, I never would have eaten it. She manipulated my naivete and my desire for her.

Lovingkindness: So, in your recollection, you bore no responsibility for your part in that incident?

Adam: No. It was all my wife's fault.

Lovingkindness: The crime report records your and Eve's eviction from Eden as a consequence of your theft of the Tree of Knowledge fruit. Are you familiar with that report?

Adam: Yes, I have read it.

Lovingkindness: Would you please read the following excerpt from that report, which is also the official transcript of God's discussion with the Celestial Council about the reasons for your eviction?

Adam *(reading):* "And the Lord God said, 'Now that the man has become like one of us, knowing good and bad, what if he should stretch out his hand and take also from the tree of life and eat, and live forever!'" (Gen. 3:22).

Lovingkindness: According to this record, God and the council evicted you and Eve from Eden to prevent the two of you from using your newfound knowledge to acquire access to eternal life. Otherwise, both of you would have violated the boundaries between humans and God. Is that your understanding?

Adam: I ate some of the Knowledge Tree fruit and I got a little smarter. They overreacted.

Lovingkindness: So, in your view, your expulsion was unnecessary. What did God and the council say specifically about you—not Eve—on the day of your eviction?

Adam: The council? You and opposing counsel *are* the council. You were there.

Lovingkindness: Please tell the jury what they said.

Adam: They—you—were talking within earshot of me. You kept looking at me and shaking your heads. . . . I distinctly recall your saying, *"The man used to be one of us. He is a colossal disappointment."* You kept saying this straight to my face, over and over. By the way, you did *not* say, *"The man has become one of us,"* as the crime report erroneously records.

Lovingkindness: Did this experience compound the trauma of being evicted from Eden?

Adam: I appreciate your rubbing the salt into my wounds.

Lovingkindness: Your son, Cain . . .

Adam: He is not technically my son.

Lovingkindness: Granted. Cain is also a farmer. Does he work with you?

Adam: We own and work farmland together. He has been more of a hindrance than a help to me.

Lovingkindness: Given the extreme difficulties of your profession, why do you think he became a farmer?

Adam: I have no idea.

Lovingkindness: Nonetheless, could you speculate as to why he would go into the farming business with you, given its lack of profitability?

Adam: I suppose he was interested in helping out the family business, to get us on our feet outside of Eden.

Lovingkindness: He could have done that by working in livestock with his brother.

Adam: They did not see eye to eye. To be more exact, Cain saw Abel as his personal black eye.

Lovingkindness: But Cain could have started his own shepherding business or gone into textiles, perhaps processing wool, correct?

Adam: I guess so.

Lovingkindness: So, I must ask again, why do you think he went into business specifically with *you*?

Adam: Maybe he wanted my attention. Maybe he had something to prove.

Lovingkindness: Maybe. Do you like Cain?

Adam: He is my wife's son. Like doesn't enter the picture here.

Lovingkindness: Do you love Cain?

Adam: He murdered my son. I am responsible for him as family, but I hate him.

Lovingkindness: How did you feel about him before the murder?

Adam: Why do you care how I felt about him? *He* is on trial, not me.

Lovingkindness: You need to answer the questions posed by this court. Let me rephrase. How did you feel about co-raising a child who was born of your wife's affair with her lover?

Adam: (no answer)

Lovingkindness: Was Cain a colossal disappointment to you? Was he someone to disown, like God tried to disown you, a colossal disappointment, during your eviction?

Adam: I am done.

Judge Ne'elam: The witness is instructed to answer the question.

Adam: All right. He was worse than a colossal disappointment.

Lovingkindness: Did you keep saying this to Cain, like God and the council kept saying it to you?

Adam: After the eviction, I mostly stopped talking. I was severely depressed. Cain kept babbling at me, trying to get me to engage with him.

Lovingkindness: Based on how God made you feel and your later reactions to Cain, would you surmise that Cain got the message from you that he was worse than a colossal disappointment?

Adam: Shit rolls downhill.

Lovingkindness: Your infelicitous remark notwithstanding, did this create a tense atmosphere in your home, especially between the two brothers?

Adam: It was not tense; it was toxic.

Lovingkindness: I see. Toxic enough to make Cain severely depressed?

Adam: I don't really know. He and I almost never spoke.

Lovingkindness: Isn't it likely that Cain felt great emotional distress at the time of the "offerings" incident?

Adam: Even if he did, did that justify his beating Abel's head into a bloody pulp?

Lovingkindness: I am asking a different question. Was the atmosphere in your family toxic enough to make Cain feel threatened by Abel, even if that threat was unfounded?

Adam: I guess so.

Lovingkindness: Thank you, Adam. Your Honor, I have no more questions for this witness.

Judge Ne'elam: Adam, you may step down from the witness stand.

Adam *(raises his right fist menacingly as he steps down, then moves toward the Defense counsel bench)*: How dare you say that Cain's distress justified his murdering my son!

(The sergeant-at-arms grabs Adam by his arm and leads him away from Lovingkindness.)

Adam *(struggling as he is being forcibly removed from the courtroom)*: How is this possibly justice? Are we all supposed to pity poor Cain? My son is dead.

Commentary on Adam's Testimony

As the sergeant-at-arms leads Adam away, Adam's eyes are obsidian flames. He is already 130 years old, battered by poverty and a near-dead farming business; a miserable marriage; infidelity; a relentless, inscrutable God Who has made impossible demands; a dead son; and his wife's son being on trial for murdering his own child.

On the first day of the trial, we speculated that Adam had been emotionally traumatized when he was expelled from Eden. Adam's testimony reveals an even more devastating experience preceding the expulsion: God's deep disappointment in him. Adam was so wounded by God's rejection and his own "fall from grace" that he inflicted that wound on Cain, thus spreading self-destructive rage and anguish to a new generation. What if Adam had channeled his devastation into self-awareness, compassion, and wisdom, and handed his sons a radically different legacy? What would *we* look like now?

The Defense knows that God rejected Adam, based on evidence from our expert witnesses, the Rabbis of the midrashic tradition. Let's look again at the verse Adam was asked to read in court: "And the Lord God said, 'Now that the man *has become like* one of us, knowing good and bad, what if he should stretch out his hand and take also from the tree of life and eat, and live forever!'" (Gen. 3:22). The midrashic Sages read what God and the other angels said to Adam in a creatively distorted manner: "The man *used to be* like one of us." Their alternate translation adapts the somewhat ambiguous Hebrew words "*Hen ha-Adam hayyah k'ahad mimenu*," which in English could be read either in the future tense or in the past tense.

A simple, *peshat*, reading of this Torah verse reveals that God removed Adam and company from Eden out of fear for the future. Having eaten from the Tree of Knowledge, the first family would overreach, go after the fruit of the Tree of Eternal Life, and subsequently become God's competitive equals or even superiors: "The man will become like one of us." Yet, the midrashic reading tells another, equally compelling, story. Created to serve as God's stewards overseeing the world, Eve and Adam were taken down by their own rebellious arrogance. Stunned and embittered by their betrayal, God cast them out of Eden. Imagine the inexperienced Parent-Partner God shrieking a grief-stricken wail in front of God's angelic entourage: "Adam was one of us! I had much greater plans for him and Eve. How could he do this to us?"[10]

Experiencing God's deep disappointment horribly scarred Adam. The trial transcript suggests that God never intended that disappointment to be a death sentence, but a demand of Adam that he learn from his and Eve's mistakes. Instead, Adam nursed his self-loathing until he found a "fall guy"—a boy not his own, onto whom he could project his self-hatred. In this sense, Cain was all too much Adam's spiritual child, who also found it comforting to inflict his hatred on Abel rather than learn from God's urgent warnings. Trauma, anger, resentment, fear, and self-loathing traveled up the first family's tree as they traveled down through its early generations.

Bearing this in mind, it is easier for us, the jury, to now understand Eve and Adam's seeming absence from the crime report. As Truth explained in the forensic assessment and as the parents insisted in their testimony, they *were* there with their sons, every agonizing step of the way. Yet, to convey the depth of Cain's culpability as a free adult, Eve and Adam's voices *had* to be muted, even silenced. God suppressed their presence in the crime report to teach Cain (and us) that, from birth to death, being your brother's keeper is an unconditional adult imperative, regardless of your childhood influences, be they an abusive parent, feeling like a victim in your family, or even more elemental sibling rage and rivalry. Your precarious perch on the family tree deserves compassion, but it never gives you the right to push someone else off its branches. By leaving Eve and Adam out of their children's story, God forces us, as it were, to place ourselves fully inside it. We stop being merely readers or observers or jurors; this is now *our story.* Left alone with Cain and his dead brother, stripped as it were of our nuclear and societal parents, *we* become siblings in every sense of that familial term: nuclear, extended, communal, human. *We,* as individuals and communities, are standing in that field with Cain and Abel as Cain lifts that rock over Abel's head. *We* inherit the fatal tribal scars from that blunt and bloody weapon of our ancestors, who in a deeply poetic sense inherited them from the first family. *We* are forced to accept this ugliest, most redemptive truth: Each time one of us projects our internal anguish onto someone else; each time one people fixates on, scapegoats, or demonizes another people perceived to be different or threatening, instead of looking more critically at themselves, Eve and Adam the bereaved parents bury Abel anew, and God shakes God's head, muttering "How could you?"[11]

The third day of the trial is coming to an end. As with their son and with Sin, we now know much more about Eve and Adam: their broken marriage, indiscretions, and unhealed hatreds that became their parental legacies. We know that Eve was torn between her horror at Cain's murderous behavior and her fierce loyalty to him. We know that Adam rejected and scarred Cain, just like Adam believed God had rejected and scarred him. We know these things, but are we any wiser about how to raise our own families, about how to be brothers and sisters?

Tomorrow, a dead silence hiding beneath these noisy proceedings will finally end. The murder victim will speak. How can this be?

$$9$$

Day Four of the Trial

On day four of the trial the court will hear the victim impact statement recorded from the blood of Abel.

A Statement by the Blood of Abel
Adamson (Recording)

Clerk: All rise. The Celestial Court is now in session. Judge Ne'elam presiding. Please be seated.

Judge Ne'elam: Good morning, ladies and gentlemen. Calling this fourth day of the case of *Cain v. Abel*. Are both sides ready?

Lovingkindness: Ready for the Defense, Your Honor.

Truth: Ready for the Prosecution, Your Honor.

Judge Ne'elam: It is standard procedure for this court to hear victim impact statements, both to determine the nature of a defendant's sentencing and to show the defendant the damage his or her crimes have had upon the victim and the community. I am in possession of a most unusual victim impact statement: Abel Adamson's. His statement comes to us in the form of a digital recording. We read in the crime report that Abel's blood cried out from the ground to God. In preparation for this proceeding, the Prosecution returned to the scene of the crime and found Abel's blood still present there, crying out.

Lovingkindness *(rising)*: Excuse me, Your Honor, but how can this court be certain of these facts? How could Abel's blood continue to cry out so long after the event in question?

Judge Ne'elam: Why Abel's blood was still present and crying out is not the primary issue before this court. We did learn from the crime report that the ground had opened its mouth and received Abel's blood from Cain's hand, thus becoming perpetually cursed (Gen. 4:11–12). The Prosecution recorded Abel's blood's statement and entered it into evidence, and as far as I am concerned that is sufficient for us to proceed. Will the clerk please play the recording?

Clerk: Yes, Your Honor. May I warn the court that Abel's blood is crying out throughout this recording? It is loud, piercing, and next to impossible to modulate.

Judge Ne'elam: Thank you. This court has been forewarned. Please play the recording.

Clerk: Yes, Your honor. *(Clerk presses buttons on a court-approved laptop.)*

Abel's Blood *(coming through loudly via speakers onstage)*: Your Honor, it is my wish to tell the court how Cain's brutality has affected me, our family, and our family's descendants. I also request up front that Cain's punishment be modified by considerations for our family background that negatively affected us both. From the time we were two living brothers until the moment Cain murdered me, the spotlight has shone solely on Cain. The crime report gives the court the erroneous impression that, while I was alive, my voice was never heard. A person reading it would think that not a word had ever passed my lips about life with my brother and my parents and what it meant to live in our miserable hovel just outside the walls of Eden. I admit, with the pall of unremitting anger and sadness thrown over our family, an anxious silence had grown inside me, a kind of mutism. I was barely able to speak beyond sporadic one-word responses, but still I spoke. Nonetheless, I have been cast as some prop for my big brother's "big story that shaped the world," one small part of which was the tale about my own death.

I was not a merely a shepherd. I was not blood spurting out of a lifeless bag of skin. I was not a crime statistic. I was not a hollow symbol for victimhood. I was a human being who was tortured by a living death before winding up as a corpse in a field.

My name, the only one I ever knew, should have been a hint to me of what my family thought of me. In their minds I was—I am—Hevel, my original Hebrew name from which you derive the English name, Abel. *Hevel:* "wind, breath, vapor, nothingness, vanity." According to the crime report, there is no indication that my parents even bothered to name me explicitly, at least not in the joyous way that Eve named Cain, and would it have mattered if they had? After all, what parents give their child a name that literally means "nothing"?

I want to explain what happened the day Cain was born. Adam, our father, was nowhere to be found, as the crime report implies. The midwife who birthed me told me that Eve our mother gave birth alone. Our distracted, overburdened, emotionally broken father had abandoned her with excuses about working the impoverished produce on land that had already been cursed by God. Between relentless contractions, Eve kept howling about Adam and an angel, something about lovers and a family damned by tainted blood. It all sounded crazy to the midwife, but as I grew up, it gradually became one missing piece to our family's puzzle. Yes, my brother was treated like some divine being, at least by my mother. Yes, she did have an affair with an actual divine being. She was fiercely determined to perpetuate our family after our expulsion, but our father was too disengaged from her, so she slept with one of the demi-gods roaming around the earth. When I got a bit older, the midwife wrote to me, "Abel, after your parents ate from the Tree of Knowledge, Samael the angel rode into their new home outside of Eden on Naḥash, the snake, then seduced your mother. When your father found out about this, he waited until after Cain was born, then he forced her to sleep with him as well." That makes sense, considering our mother's relationship with that snake back in Eden, but who really knows?

I do know that when Cain burst out of her womb, smothered in blood and amniotic fluid and screaming air out of his lusty, tiny lungs, our mother was consumed by cathartic relief and joy that she had created her own version of immortality: "*Kaniti ish et adonai!* [I have gained a male child with the help of the Lord!]" (Gen. 4:1).

I don't blame my father for wanting to have nothing do with this bastard whom he was now obligated to treat as a son. With the actual father nowhere to be found, Adam became responsible for Cain, yet his ugly sense of betrayal and humiliation distorted their relationship. He spent the rest of his life hating and mistreating my brother. He also spent his life alternately despising and desiring my mother. I was conceived and born from their sickening relationship — not a bastard child, but the poisoned progeny of two people whose lives together had long since corroded.

My mother's words always made clear to me that she loved my brother with a fierce, primitive intensity she would never feel for me. Imagine the desperation, then the disgust, she must have felt at the moments of my conception and birth. While Cain, her first fruit, bounced on her knee, she would lose herself in the delirium of maternal love. The midwife later told me just how different it was when I came along. The day I kicked my way out of her, screaming as loudly as my sibling, desperate to be swaddled, held, loved, welcomed, all she could say was, "Shut it up!" And so I, Hevel, the "nothing man,"[1] entered the world, my self-hatred incessantly muffling me to make mommy happy, until the day I died.

I do not doubt that a part of Eve loved me; it was just the much smaller part of her capacity to love. My brother had nothing less than mommy's full, unthinking devotion. But that wasn't enough for him. He wanted nothing more than daddy's approval, and daddy couldn't or wouldn't give it to him.

Meanwhile, I—mostly ignored by my parents—actually felt a great deal of compassion for Cain. He was *lahut ahar ha-adamah*, burning with passion for farming the land, that one fragile, cursed endeavor he had in common with our father.[2] How desperately he tried to get our father's attention, and how it backfired. Daddy was forced to farm for our family's survival, and he hated it. He coaxed almost nothing from the poisoned ground except thorns and thistles. He despised Cain for clinging, puppy-like, to him as they trudged out together in the early morning darkness, hoes and sickles across their shoulders.

I was lonely in those days, but I was safe.

I've heard the allegations that our mother gave birth to three daughters during the times she bore us,[3] but it's not true. There were only four of us then: my parents; my angry, entitled, bruised brother; and me. Each morning I pastured our flock in the fields well beyond my father's miserable land plots, and each evening I drove the flock back into the sheep pens, closed the gates, and lay down to sleep. Being practically invisible to my family had its advantages, for it gave me the freedom to stay out of their pathological relationship. I could feel resentment some days, but more than anything I felt relief at being left alone.

By the time Cain and I were forty-one and forty years old, respectively, I had become a wealthy shepherd, while Cain's farming career continued to languish. I cannot assume credit for my good fortune. Certainly, I was diligent, yet I was mostly lucky. The wild grass near our homestead was plentiful and hardy, my sheep would eat all day, the flocks fattened, and their teats would practically burst with milk. A robust flock of sheep produces more robust flocks of sheep, and so I consoled my quiet, lonely self with the twin satisfactions of work and wealth.

Just as he was unsuccessful at getting our father to love him, Cain was unsuccessful as a farmer. And so the day came when, frustrated by his relationships with land and family, he began to hound me with questions about how I had done so well with my sheep. "It doesn't add up," he confronted me. "I've worked so much harder than you. How have you done so well for yourself?"

The way he leered at me with that look of befuddled jealousy frightened me. "Luck?" I mumbled back to him, hoping he'd be satisfied with my one-word answer. It only whetted his need to ask me more questions.

Eve still did the adult equivalent of petting his head and reminding Cain he was the favored child, but her ardor for "number one son" was cooling with old age. Adam barely looked at Cain anymore. I wanted to shake Cain's stupid carcass and tell him to stop acting like an emotional slob. He would never make Daddy happy. Adam would never truly love any of us. He was damaged goods. Of course, I kept my mouth shut, which for me was already very easy.

Things were way too hard for our parents. Cain had such a limited perspective, but I recognized our mother and father's limitations. After all, they themselves had never had human parents, only God. They'd never had the benefit of growing up with other humans who could model good behavior for them and help them figure out actions and consequences. Instead, God had directed them to tend Eden almost as soon as they had begun to breathe: "Reproduce!, populate!, master the land!, name the animals!, work the earth!, guard the grounds!, eat this!, don't eat that!, don't eat from that fruit tree in the middle of Eden!, if you eat from it you will die!" (Gen. 1:28–30, 2:15–17, 2:19–20).

Being God's partners in supervising the earth was an admittedly honorable task, but it was also perilously premature. They had no clue how to be each other's partner, how to enjoy each other sexually, how to resist temptation, how to raise kids, how to build a family and hold down demanding jobs for an impossible boss, notwithstanding God's declarations about creating our mother to be our father's fitting helper (Gen. 2:18).

Cain saw none of this. He was a grown man forever trotting out his list of grievances against our parents, the earth, and me.

He badgered me repeatedly: "Abel, how about a friendly competition? Let's you and I offer our best to God. We'll see whose gifts God judges to be better." This was obviously a bad idea. Did Cain think this way he would finally get that parental love he craved from God? He knew I was more professionally successful than he was, so why did he think he was going to win? For me, even if I won, there was no outcome in which I could walk away the actual winner. And I didn't want to be a winner; I just wanted to be left alone.

I tried over and over to get him to let it go. He wouldn't let up. One day, just to get him away from me, I uttered, "Okay."

We built two altars. We each brought the fruits of our respective cultivations and turned them into burned offerings. Just as I had suspected, the flax Cain brought to please God and reclaim his sense of purpose and dignity was no match for the fat ewe I offered.

Cain's offering is mentioned first in the crime record. That was because he was beside himself with anxiety to get God to pay attention to him. He was desperate for God's love and my regard. Sadly, he did not understand that, even if he won this contest, it would not change God's esteem for him—or mine, for that matter.

He did the best he could, but the earth's curse—our father's curse—damned him. And just as I'd feared, God paid no heed to him as a flame from heaven descended and licked my fat little ewe right off the altar (Gen. 4:4–5). God took the damage our parents dumped on Cain and me and made it worse.

"*Lama naflu fanekha?*," God questioned him after our contest was over. "Why has your face fallen?" This was no mere metaphor: His facial muscles literally drooped from the weight of rage and sadness upon him.

I remember being troubled by God's response to Cain's anguish. After rejecting his offering for no discernible purpose, and then seeing the unmistakable fury in Cain's dark look, rather than comfort him, God gave him a warning about not letting his hurt affect his behavior: "Sin crouches at the door . . . yet you can be its master" (Gen. 4:8).

I knew I had to get out of the way of that fire. I tried to lay low, to avoid Cain, to appease him, to reason with him, but I failed, fatally.

I was grazing my sheep in the high noon sun, my dog faithfully at my side.[4] The heat was making me drowsy, but I kept telling myself, *Stay awake!* Suddenly, Cain was upon me. He held his hoe in one hand and a jagged, pointy rock in the other. I squinted in the sun, felt a flash of horror, and whispered to him, "Cain?"

"Brother, God wants the best. So now I will offer God what pleases God the most."

In less than the duration of a breath I was dead, and my blood was soaking into the earth.

And it was then, paradoxically, that I found my voice and my power, my loud, relentless demand for justice.

Your Honor, I wish to address my brother. Cain, I will always have empathy for you, for you too were a victim of the cruelties of circumstance. Yet, I can never truly forgive you, for you chose to fight your own victimization by victimizing me. Your evil is splattered like my blood on the stones and the trees. And I too am everywhere, the father of every victim speaking up against every victimizer, refusing to have his or her mouth shut up and his or her blood buried. Every victim henceforth in the history of humanity is one of my children.

In conclusion, I turn to God. Why would You allow one human being to destroy another? You created each of us in Your image, so how could You allow Your image to be so disfigured? I know Your righteous indignation against my brother was sincere, but I've heard Your self-incrimination too, right here in the words of the crime report: "*Kol d'mei aḥikha tzo-akim* ei-lai *min ha-adamah.* [Your brother's blood cries out *to* Me from the ground]" (Gen. 4:10). With a change of one small Hebrew letter, that Hebrew word, *ei-lai,* "to Me," can be vocalized in a radically different way: *ah-lai,* "against Me."[5] "*Your brother's blood cries out* against Me *from the ground.*"

Thus *You knew* that I cried out for justice—not only against Cain, but against You as well.

God, allow me to tell an old story. A king once presided over a bloody gladiatorial contest. At the very moment the victor was to slaughter the loser, the king could have raised his hands and ended the fight. Instead, the king did nothing, preferring that the battle come to its gory end.[6]

Were You not that king? Were Cain and I not the gladiators?

Some will say that You looked on in horror at the ensuing atrocities. What else could You have done, once You decided to create us morally free with sinful impulses? You had to grant us the dignity of living with the cursed blessing of choice.

But . . .

Why would You create Sin, grant Sin enormous power, set Sin loose, then feebly admonish humanity not to succumb to Sin?

Why have You never had the will to step in front of Sin and say, "Enough!"

And why have You hidden from the people of this court?

To hide from my accusations, our accusations, *You sat in that chair and presided over this trial as the Judge!*

Enough faux justice. Off with the robes, the comfort of a costume behind which You've been hiding with impunity. You, God, have posed for too long as Judge Ne'elam, so there is yet one more trial to be held: Yours.

You, God, must be called to account for Your negligence.

I demand that You answer my blood screaming from the earth this one question:

Should You, the Judge of all the earth, not have acted justly?[7]

10

Day Four Continues

By this point, everyone in the courtroom is standing up and howling at God, now exposed by Abel as the Judge Who is about to be judged. We watch, mesmerized, as God's court robe comes off, but we see only the robe; we cannot see God. We do not see God move to the witness stand, but it is clear to everyone that, as of this moment, God is the One on trial.

The Tables Turned as God Is Put on Trial

God (*directing God's voice toward the jury*)**:** Yes, I am Who you say I am. I had to remain hidden in this courtroom. Had I presided openly as Myself, Cain's trial would have turned into a referendum on *Me* and *My role* in this fratricide. You would have asked Me:

- "Why do You, God, let evil people inflict suffering upon good people?"
- "Why did You forbid Eve and Adam from eating the fruit of the Tree of Knowledge, only to shove it in their faces, then punish them for succumbing to temptation?"
- "Were You justified in paying attention to Abel but ignoring Cain?"
- "Why would You create Sin, place Sin in Cain's way, and then warn Cain about Sin, knowing Sin would consume him?"

- "Why did You allow Cain to murder Abel?"
- "Did You have no choice but to let the human drama take its free course?"
- "Shouldn't You, the Judge of all the earth, have acted justly?"

I will not give you answers—not because I don't care, not because I am cruel, not because I don't have answers, not because I am inscrutably mysterious, and *not* because I don't judge justly. I will not provide you with answers because, in the end, My answers do not matter as much as *yours*. To you I direct the same questions that Cain and I asked each other long ago in the killing field:

- "Where is your brother?"
- "Am I my brother's keeper?"
- "What have you done?!'"

Yes, it is all about *you*. The writer John Steinbeck understood this when he declared that the most important word in the world was the very one I had uttered to Cain in Hebrew in My warning: *timshol*. It means "Thou mayest," as in "Thou mayest rule over Sin." Not "Thou must." Not "Thou will." "Thou mayest." Steinbeck said:

There are many millions in their sects and churches who feel the order, "Do thou," and throw their weight into obedience. And there are millions more who feel predestination in "Thou shalt." Nothing they may do can interfere with what will be. But "Thou mayest"! Why, that makes a man great, that gives him stature with the gods, for in his weakness and his filth and his murder of his brother he has still the great choice. He can choose his course and fight it through and win.[1]

Brilliant fellow, Mr. Steinbeck, but I do not entirely agree with him.[2] Yes, freedom to rule over your darkest passions is the center of human behavior, *but it is not the center of the center.* You must always ask, freedom for what purpose?

The most important words in the world are the three words Cain asked of me:

"*Ha-shomer aḥi anokhi?* [Am I my brother's keeper?]"

And that is the one question I *will* answer for this court. Yes, you are.

Commentary on God's Testimony I: What Did Cain Really Ask God?

We tend to interpret Cain's response to God's question, "Where is Abel your brother?," as a cynical, rhetorical parry meant to avoid confrontation and responsibility, in essence, "I *do* not know; am I my brother's keeper?" In his commentary on our story, the nineteenth-century Torah scholar and educator Rabbi Meir Leibush Weisser (the Malbim) explains Cain's answer quite differently (and radically): "Cain answered God, 'I honestly *did not know* that Abel was my brother who loved me.' Cain thought that human beings have no moral freedom and cannot make their own choices."[3] According to Rabbi Weisser, Cain was not being cagey whatsoever. Cain honestly believed that the choice to help or hurt Abel was out of his hands and entirely up to God.

By contrast, in the above monologue, God reminds us that both displacement of culpability and genuine ignorance of the law are unacceptable rationales for wrongdoing. God's purported influence over our potential to be cruel and violent is mostly irrelevant. We are always our brothers' keepers. Whether or not we love or even like each other, we are "forced to be free" to take care of one another as siblings in the vast human family.

Commentary on God's Testimony II:
Preparing for Cain's Sentence

The trial is almost over. In minutes, God the Judge will finally address Cain.

What, we wonder, is fair and just punishment for his crime? Cain's guilt was easy to determine, for he confessed at the crime scene. Sentencing will be much harder.

Should Cain be put to death? Certainly, capital punishment will become a standard of retributive justice many generations later, in the world occupied by Noah's descendants after the Great Flood. Echoing God's condemnation of Cain that Abel's innocent blood cried out from the earth, God will declare to Noah and all humanity: "Whoever sheds the blood of man / By man shall his blood be shed / For in His image / Did God make man" (Gen. 9:6).[4]

Because this murder is the first of its kind, Cain's sentence will also become the paradigm on which justice for all future brutality will be modeled. Not only that: It will be a paradigm for thinking about the tortured love affair between God and humans. It will also be a framework for subsequent arguments about guilt, responsibility, punishment, repentance, forgiveness, and the worthwhileness of human existence.

After the initial sentence is pronounced, God will confer with us, the jury. *We* must give God our perspectives, for (at least) two reasons. First: Just as shedding another person's blood is a crime against God, distorting God's "face," it is also a crime against the entire human family. Second: We, the human family, will have to live with the enduring consequences of this sentence.

Our input, while not definitive, is crucial.

Sentencing of Cain

God: At this time, I ask the clerk of the court to bring the defendant forward to the Judge's bench.

(The clerk and the sergeant-at-arms instruct Cain to rise and accompany them to stand before God the Judge.)

God: Mr. Adamson, your guilt is not at issue in this court. From the outset it was clear that you murdered your brother, and in doing so erased one quarter of the world's population. What has always concerned this court is the extent of your guilt, for that is key to your sentencing.

The Prosecution has painted you as an arrogant, amoral man who killed your brother believing you were entitled to supremacy over him. The Defense has portrayed you as a hardworking man beaten up by life's injustices who killed your brother out of outrage and deep hurt that I favored him unfairly over you. You have been alternatively described as cold and hot, calculating and impulsive, unfeeling and overheated. Sin said it was easy to convince you that you were the real victim and that your crime was an act of self-defense.

Cain, regardless of why you murdered Abel, it was still fratricide. If you murdered him out of rage, frustration, and the belief that he got what was rightly yours, it was fratricide. If life was unfair to you, you still had no right to let your worst passions control you and rob him of the most precious thing I ever gave him or you. When you shed the blood of another person, you distorted My image. You disfigured Me.

By all rights, I should sentence you to death at the hands of your peers. However, this sentence is problematic at best. You had no prior warning or full understanding of murder and its consequences. Even more importantly, perhaps, meting out this form of justice, unchecked by mercy, may become a backdoor through which blind revenge and hatred walk easily and blithely. How readily injustice can be dressed as righteousness.

Mercy unchecked by justice would be just as distortive and unjust. As much compassion as I feel for your suffering, and whatever remorse I feel for My likely contributions to that suffering, Abel was the only true victim in this crime. You must be punished for destroying him and his potential progeny.

The balance of justice and mercy is a spiritually radioactive isotope: Nothing is more unstable and fraught. Nonetheless, it is necessary for the perpetuation of humanity.

And so, I pronounce your most appropriate punishment: sparing your life but compelling you to a life that is less than a life.

Mr. Adamson, please remain standing. The clerk will now read aloud the various aggravating and mitigating circumstances to which I have given weight in determining your sentence. Your official sentence will follow.

Clerk (*rising, approaching the Judge's bench, and reading from, among other manuscripts, the original copy of God's crime report*): The verdict in this case is already known to the court. On Nisan 14, 0041, the defendant, Cain Adamson, entered a plea of guilty for the first-degree murder of his brother, Abel. Today, the 24th of Nisan, 0041, we proceed with his sentencing. During the trial, this court has heard many expert witnesses testify as to why the defendant murdered his brother. Among all the explanations discussed in court, the following factors have been accounted for, along a continuum from "Light" to "Great" weight, in determining the defendant's sentence, as follows:

AGGRAVATING FACTORS

- The capital felony was a homicide. — Great weight
- God personally warned the defendant that his capitulation to Sin would lead to grave, albeit undefined, behavioral consequences. — Moderate weight

- On being confronted by God at the crime scene, the defendant appeared to refuse to take responsibility for his actions. —Great weight
- It is possible that the defendant is unremorseful for his actions. —Moderate weight
- An instructive example needs to be made of the defendant for the sake of civilization. —Great weight

MITIGATING FACTORS

- The defendant's family life adversely influenced his ability to rationally assess and conduct his relationships with all those around him, including himself. —Little to moderate weight
- The defendant was operating under the powerful influences of emotional distress and Sin's manipulative interventions. —Moderate weight
- The defendant had no personal or societal precedents that would have helped him to form a judgment about murder as an illegal act. —Great weight
- God's warning to the defendant about his future behavior and its consequences may have been too vague and inexplicit for him to internalize. —Moderate weight
- It is possible that the defendant is genuinely remorseful for his actions. —Moderate weight
- An instructive example needs to be made of the defendant for the sake of civilization. —Great weight[5]

(The clerk now looks up from the paper, to the crowd, and then turns to a new paper entitled "Sentence of Cain." The crowd sees this. There is an audible collective intake of breath as the clerk reads the forthcoming words: "It is the judgment of this court...")

Clerk: It is the judgment of this court:

For the murder of Abel Adamson, the defendant is to be cursed more than the ground that received his brother's blood.

He shall be a ceaseless wanderer in exile upon the face of the earth.

He shall till the soil and it shall no longer yield its strength to him.

He shall be banished this day from the soil.

He must avoid God's protecting presence.

He shall be subject to the whims of all those he meets, both humans and animals. Anyone who meets him may kill him.

He shall be provided with a protective mark, lest anyone who meets him tries to kill him.

He shall do hard labor by building a new city for the purposes of future human habitation. He will found that city and name it after his son, Enoch.

He is prohibited from living in that city, for he is already subject to ceaseless wandering and exile. (Taken from Gen. 4:11–15)

God *(turning to Cain)*: In other words, Mr. Adamson, you are to remain alive, but you will be exiled and marginalized. As such you shall forever be a moral and punitive example for others. Having brought death into the world, you will foster civilization and life through the building of a new city as a form of restorative justice.

(The sentencing announcements are interrupted by shouts of frustration and anger within the courtroom. Both Truth and Lovingkindness are shocked and dismayed. Truth had wanted Cain put to death; Lovingkindness had wanted to see him rehabilitated. Kill him or let him return to society such as it is, but exile? "Too much left unresolved, a public safety and policy nightmare in the making," they mutter, intentionally out of God's hearing, but just perceptibly loud enough for we the jury to make out their unified chorus.)

God: These proceedings will not continue until there is silence. *(The courtroom goes quiet.)* Thank you. *(Looking intently at Cain).* Mr.

Adamson, you have one last opportunity to speak in this court. Have you reflected on your behavior? Do you feel any contrition for your actions?

Cain: (*No response. Cain takes a tentative step forward, then falls backward, crumbling to the floor. From his violently shaking hand, a grimy copy of the crime report falls, one sentence of the transcript circled thickly in blood red: "Gadol avoni min'so." ["My sin is too great to bear. My punishment is too great to bear."]*)

God (*to the courtroom at large*): Please maintain silence in the courtroom while I confer with the jury. Because Cain's crime is against the entire human family, and will forever affect the human family, I would like the jury to weigh in on his sentencing.

(*The courtroom remains hushed as God spends several minutes conferring privately with us, the jury. God then publicly addresses the court.*)

God (*publicly to the jury*): Do you wish to offer a suggestion regarding the sentence I issued today?

Jury: Your Honor, we wish to add a recommendation about the protective mark You will be placing on Cain to protect him from others who might otherwise kill him in exile. Perhaps you are considering such signs as a horn, a guard dog, fear instilled in the hearts of other people and animals, the sun, or skin disease.[6] We are hoping You might be open to something else.

God: What kind of mark do you have in mind?

Jury: A mirror, Your Honor. We would like the mark of Cain to be mirrors. This way, every time one of us encounters Cain, we will stop. We will look closely and see a reflection . . . of ourselves.

God: I will grant your request. May it only be that you see what stands before you.

11

Beyond Cain

The trial having concluded, Cain now leaves God's Presence, outfitted with mirrors from the top to the bottom of his body. Some humans he will encounter may see Cain reflected in their own images and think more honestly about themselves. Others will see only their own images and fall in love with themselves. Exile, its dangers and possibilities, await Cain, but we wonder: After Abel's death, does Cain's life have an afterlife?

The Torah tells us that after he leaves God's Presence, Cain settles in the land of Nod (Gen. 4:17). He marries (Gen. 4:17). He has a son, Enoch (Gen. 4:17). He builds a city and names it after his son (Gen. 4:17). This is a bizarre postscript to being sentenced to wander in exile. How does a criminal so condemned by God settle anywhere permanently, marry, have a child, and build a city? We cannot conclude that Cain's exile is an internal experience of psychic suffering, for the Torah is clear: God makes Cain *literally* wander, neither fully alive nor fully dead, spared the death penalty but burdened with homelessness of mind and body.

Fortunately, our expert witnesses of the ancient midrashic commentary on Genesis are able to fill in various missing textual details between the time of the sentencing and Cain's setting foot back on the ground that drank Abel's blood. According to Genesis 4:16, "Cain left the presence of the Lord and settled in the land of Nod, east of

Eden." Rabbi Ḥinena bar Yitzḥak, a fourth-century CE Sage from the Land of Israel, supplies an imaginative description of what was happening to Cain when he left God's presence:

> Cain left God's presence a happy man, because he sincerely repented and God forgave him. When God condemned Cain to exile, Cain cried out, *"Is my sin too great to bear?"* (Gen. 4:13). Master of the universe, If You can tolerate the sinfulness of the entire world, how could my sinfulness be too great for You to also tolerate?" God responded to Cain, "Because you confessed to doing wrong (by calling your behavior sinful), you have repented. Go now into exile from this place, for it is exile that atones for sinful behavior." As he was leaving, he met his father, Adam, who asked him, "How did you fare in your sentencing?" Cain answered him, "I repented, and God and I reconciled."[1]

The significance of this testimony becomes increasingly clear with one more transcript. This post-trial recording is the present author's midrashic expansion on Rabbi Ḥinena's teaching.

Adam: Why the silence in court?

Cain: You cut me off, choking me with your silence for decades, and you ask me about *my* silence?

Adam: You could have set your own record straight. Why the silence? Was it trauma or trickery?

Cain: Tinnitus.

Adam: Stop it. Be honest with me about why you didn't open your mouth in court. Your mother and I would have lived through it. We lived through the murder; we could live through anything.

Cain: I told you, tinnitus. Abel's screaming blood has been ringing in my ears since that day. No matter what I try to say, it gets drowned out *and* exacerbates the ringing. The only way I could remain composed in court was to keep my mouth shut.

Adam (*noticing the same half-crooked smile on Cain's face as he wore on the first day of the trial*): What is so funny? You murdered your brother.

Cain: I am smiling because I repented, and God forgave me.

Adam: Did you convert out of conviction? Or out of the conviction that it could lessen your conviction?

Cain: All that matters is that I repented and God forgave me. It does not make me any less of a murderer, but it makes me more of a human being. If God could forgive me for murdering my brother, maybe you can forgive me for murdering your son? I did a monstrous thing, murdering Abel. All I can do is beg forgiveness, maybe do a little better tomorrow than today.

Adam: I think that God had *empathy* for you. Empathy is not forgiveness. God never forgave me either, I think. I know for sure that God crapped on me, I crapped on you, you crapped on your brother. There's shame in all of it.

Cain: I agree. And that's why, once I walk away from you, I won't look back at you and my mother. I refuse to look back at what I can't change. I'm only looking forward, toward the endless stretches of desert beyond Eden, toward rebuilding the life I destroyed after I brutally murdered Abel.

Commentary on Cain in Exile: Cain Rebuilds

The Torah narrates that, after his exile east of Eden, Cain and his progeny waste no time in building some of the foundations of civilization:

> Cain knew his wife, and she conceived and bore Enoch. And he then founded a city and named the city after his son Enoch. To Enoch was born Irad, and Irad begot Mehujael, and Mehujael begot Methusael, and Methusael begot Lamech. Lamech took to himself two wives: the name of the one was Adah and the name of the other was Zillah. Adah bore Jabal; he was the ancestor of those who dwell in tents and amidst herds. And the name of his brother was Jubal; he was the ancestor of all who play the lyre

and the pipe. As for Zillah, she bore Tubal-cain, who forged all implements of copper and iron. And the sister of Tubal-cain was Naamah. (Gen. 4:17–22)

Cain's attempt to rebuild life after his act of destruction is a mixed bag of hope and unrepentant self-interest, but an attempt to rebuild nonetheless. It is intensified by the Torah text that shows up toward the end of Genesis. Suddenly, after a long absence, Eve and Adam reappear in the text, ready to hope in life again: "Adam knew his wife again, and she bore a son and named him Seth, meaning, 'God has provided me with another offspring in place of Abel,' for Cain had killed him" (Gen. 4:25).

This verse comes a few verses after a genealogical list recounted in Genesis 4:17–22, just beyond our immediate story. We might expect it to follow right after the Cain and Abel story, but, instead, it materializes right after a strange story fragment about Lamech, Cain's sixth-generation descendant, and his two wives:

And Lamech said to his wives,
"Adah and Zillah, hear my voice;
O wives of Lamech, give ear to my speech.
I have slain a man for wounding me,
And a lad for bruising me.
If Cain is avenged sevenfold,
Then Lamech seventy-sevenfold." (Gen 4:23–24)

These verses imply that Lamech loves to crow about his violent behavior, so perhaps this verse about Eve and Adam's new child, Seth, is well placed here. Its theme of new life, especially after fratricide, seems to be a direct response to Lamech's obsession with violence and death.

The Sages of different midrashic traditions notice an even more violent and tragic connection between Lamech, his ancestor Cain, and Seth's birth to Eve and Adam. They wonder—as all of us might—

what ultimately happened after Cain repented, went into exile, and rebuilt his life. Did he ever see his parents again? Did he ever meet his new brother? How far can—and does—repentance go in promoting reconciliation in any family, after one of its members has traumatized that family? They teach the following about Cain's fate:[2]

How did Cain die? For 130 years he wandered to and fro under God's curse. His descendant, Lamech, was a blind hunter. He hunted with his son, Tubal-cain, holding his hand. Whenever the boy saw an animal, he told Lamech and Lamech hunted it down. One day, Tubal-cain mistook Cain for a beast, saying, "I see a wild animal." Lamech shot his arrow and hit the target. When the boy described the man with a mark on his forehead lying dead before them, Lamech wailed in grief, "I killed grandpa!" He clapped his hands together so hard he struck Tubal-cain, killing him by accident. . . . When he returned home without ancestor and child, he commanded (his wives) Adah and Zillah, "Lie with me (in order to procreate again.)" They responded, "You killed our ancestor (Cain) and our son (Tubal-cain). Why should we get pregnant under the cloud of your curse?" Lamech replied, "Let us go to Adam to judge." Adam told Adah and Zillah, "Submit to your husband's wish (and make new children)." "Hypocrite!" they said, "You and Eve have been celibate for 130 years since Abel died. You stayed knowingly apart from her" (to avoid having children). On hearing this, Adam desired and knew his wife again. . . . (This is why Eve and Adam gave birth to Seth.)[3]

Note the ironic circularity of the story. Cain, the murderer of one quarter of the world's population, meets his end at the hands of his descendant, Lamech, who also inadvertently kills one quarter of his own descendants.[4] This aspect of the legend emphasizes the Rabbinic idea of *middah k'neged middah*, "measure for measure." As Cain did to Abel, so did Lamech to him.

The story now returns to the first couple.

THE SIGNIFICANCE OF SETH

Eve and Adam go on to bear Seth, and in a sense, Seth redeems Abel from death. These founding parents, the ones we would have thought least likely to revive a dying, violence-riddled human race, are the ones who discover a new sense of existential urgency and sexual vigor, then make love and bear Seth as the literal replacement for Abel. Seth saves all future generations from the trauma of fratricide by serving as the bridge to the new human lineage, which, through the family of Noah, will populate and repopulate the world.

Taken together with these interpretations, Genesis 4:25 can be understood as more than an incidental fragment in the book's early genealogy of the human race. Following so many stories about the calamities resulting from human desires for sex, power, and esteem, this verse returns Eve and Adam — and us — to sexual intimacy and reproduction. This is a potent, hope-filled response to anguish. Somehow, despite — or perhaps because of — the tragic dissolution of their family, our first parents manage to find each other once again in the mystery of sex and love, and rebuild their family. Eve and Adam use physical and emotional desires for each other to fight despair. They refuse to allow their grief to destroy them and, by extension, humanity.

The Torah alludes to this legacy of hope and life by making Seth the new founder of the human race. The second report of Seth's birth records a new genealogy of Adam's family, one that leaves Cain and Abel out altogether: "This is the record of Adam's line. . . . When Adam had lived 130 years, he begot a son in his likeness after his image, and he named him Seth" (Gen. 5:1).

By offering us this alternative genealogy, perhaps the Torah is telling us that the Cain and Abel story is only *one version* of the long human story. Genesis 1:27 relates that Eve and Adam were created in God's image, as mirror reflections of the Divine. By extension or implication, so were Cain and Abel, and Cain's offspring. Yet, as Rabbi Abraham Joshua Heschel put it so aptly, at times Cain's "mark," the legacy of human nature mirrored in violence since the beginning, overshadows the divine image reflected in us.[5] With Seth's birth and the rebirth of humanity, Cain's legacy is in turn overshadowed.

In essence, the Torah may be asserting that the human capacity to love and create is an equally powerful dimension of human experience. Seth's birth posits the human capacity to relish one another, to hope, and to rebuild. While Sin is here to stay, always couching by our doors, love is one of the most potent weapons we have against the destruction we inflict on one another.

WE ARE NOAH'S CHILDREN, TOO

Furthermore, each of us may metaphorically live on as both Cain *and* Seth, a mixture of evil and good inclinations, destructiveness and redemption. Comparing the generational lists in Genesis 4 and 5, we discover two ten-generation genealogies with similarly and sometimes same-named individuals—Enoch and Enosh, Irad and Jared, Kenan and Kenan, Methusael and Methusaleh, Mehujael and Mahalalel, Lamech and Lamech—apparent evidence of strong ties between Cain's and Seth's descendants. The text seems to be hinting that the new first family's legacy mirrors the old one that has died. In fact, coming at the end of this genealogy is the birth of Noah, along with a disastrous decline of universal morality that will impel God to flood the planet and start life over (Gen. 5:1–32).

Significantly, the talmudic Rabbis do not refer to humanity as the children of Cain, Abel, or Seth, even though we have inherited all of their legacies. In Rabbinic parlance, we are *b'nei Noah*, "the children of Noah." We are distant survivor-descendants of Cain's violence, Abel's victimization, and Seth's hopefulness, but we are *direct* descendants of Noah. Noah, the only upright person living in a time of overwhelming human evil, went on to found the new human race because God deemed that he alone was sufficiently righteous to do so. Yet, as a survivor of that era, he also had one foot firmly in that old world. He wrested new life from the ashes of his generation's destructiveness, but he could never completely wash those ashes away.

More than once during this trial, we the jury have been reminded that Cain and Abel's story is merely "Exhibit A" in the "real trial," the contest between God and God's angels about that greatest question: Given our equal capacity for depravity and decency in our treatment of each other and the world, was it worth it for God to have created us at all? Clearly, God's love and hope for us were so powerful that *God* already answered that question with no intention of turning God's back on us. Even after setting Sin crouching at our doors with no rhyme or reason, even after wiping the earth clean of humanity in a fit of destructive rage, God found the strength to rebuild humanity and the world through us, Noah's descendants, bearers of the ashes of Eve, Adam, Sin, Cain, and Abel.

Truth be told, for all their fierce defense of, or opposition to, humanity, the angels' respective opinions are now irrelevant. We are here to stay, and, unlike the angels, we have to live with those legacies of Eve, Adam, Sin, Cain, and Abel. Looking in Cain's many mirrors, we see only the gritty face of being real, human, alive, pock-marked and beautiful, monstrous and magnificent, all at the same time. Angels can't see themselves in a mirror. For all their celestial beauty, they possess no earthly substance, so there is nothing to reflect back to the viewer.

All that remains of this timeless argument is us. How are *we* answering or not answering that question, as God made clear we must do? We the jury end this part of our journey with Cain and his family—our human family—in the form of two dreams. Perhaps our ability to dream something better than what happened in the killing field of Cain and Abel is all we have . . . and all we need?

Epilogue

Two Dreams

Moses' brother, Aaron, the High Priest, is the quintessential *ohev shalom, v'rodef shalom*, "lover and pursuer of peace."[1] Whenever Aaron hears of two people fighting and refusing to forgive one another, he approaches each of them with a purposeful lie. To the first he says, "I heard that so-and-so is devastated by what he did to you! He rips his clothing and beats his chest in grief, embarrassment, and regret over how he treated you, wailing, 'How can I ever face my friend again?!'" Once he appeases the first person, Aaron rushes over to tell the second one exactly the same thing. When the two later meet on the street, they fall into each other's arms and embrace, each convinced of his own rightness and the other's remorse.[2]

In our first dream, we feel righteous and sophisticated as we excoriate Aaron with questions about his peace tactics: "What kind of a diplomatic strategy is that? You're lying, manipulating people's egos, allowing them to deflect responsibility for lousy behavior, all for what? A peace founded on one sham overlapping another? Don't you think your successes are pyrrhic victories when you consider the costs to the integrities of all involved?" To this, Aaron just smiles and says, "Guilty as charged." Aaron is happy to bear the burden of the long-term costs, if it means that two human beings engaged in the most bitter conflict face each other again with love and forgiveness, if only for the briefest of seconds. To him, a world devoid of peace is a hellhole into which we dare not fall.

Our second dream is really Aaron's that we watch, but is it a dream or time travel? Aaron stumbles onto the field where Cain is wielding that sharp, heavy stone over the head of his brother. Seeing that swift downward arc of the stone in Cain's sunburned hand, Aaron speedily jumps into this literal hellhole. His forehead intercepts the sharpest point of the stone, which knocks him unconscious. He dreams within his dream that Abel's billions of descendants are streaming out of the gash in his head, thanking him for a precious opportunity to be born.

When he comes to, Cain and Abel are looking him over to see if he is moving, while still circling each other like hungry hyenas.

"Cain? Abel?" he whispers.

"Yes, us," they respond, hoarse, but amazingly in unison.

"Did I . . . just stop the murder?"

"Yes."

"How is it that I'm here with you?"

"We don't know. But you aren't the first to show up."

"I don't understand."

"God has never been able to undo our animosity. So every day God brings one good human being back to this killing field to stop Cain from striking the fatal blow. Every day, one person fulfills Lovingkindness's assurance to God that humans can and will be merciful and just."

"And I . . . succeeded," Aaron acknowledges, still shuddering. *How close it was.*

"Yes," Cain responds slowly. "But don't think for a moment that a brief stay in the violence will solve our problems. When you walk away, the bloodshed will continue."

Abel, true to form, nods silently in assent.

By this point, Eve and Adam have rushed to the field. So have God, Sin, every animal, angel, and human, all coming from miles and millennia to watch the pivotal scene of two brothers blessed and cursed with the enormous, endless power to choose good or evil.

The voluptuous monster Sin is beckoning seductively, "Cain! Cain!"

Aaron re-approaches Cain and Abel, who are now standing beside their parents. He says to the family, "God gave you as much power to move past your rage and violence as the power to succumb to them."

Eve and Adam: "We'll do anything to head off these boys' violence."

Abel: "Anything to keep from dying with a rock to my head."

Cain: "Nothing will make a difference, but go ahead."

Aaron proceeds to ask questions and listen to what the poet Stephen Dobyns calls the "Long Story":[3] of Eve and Adam's failed quest for divinity and expulsion from paradise; of Abel's innocent, frustrating favor; of Cain's ambition, depression, anger, self-pity, and self-justification. Each of them has a narrative that needs to be heard.

Time and again, one of them tries to challenge, cut off, trivialize, or recast the story of another. Aaron looks at that person, gently asks for quiet, and tells the narrator, "Please keep going."

Seconds stretch into minutes, hours, or is it days, weeks, months, years, decades, centuries, millennia, forever? The substance, the accuracy of one account compared to another, all this is less important than the fact that everyone must listen to everyone else. Is it possible that the more they listen to each other, the more they will understand each other? The pain, anger, desire to murder will not be extirpated, but just maybe it will be subdued, replaced by a sense of common experience, compassion, empathy.

"Cain! Cain!," Sin is still beckoning, "Remember what I told you that day at Abel's sheep pen, as you kicked in the door? 'You can be *its* master.' That Abel is nothing more than an *it*, a mere exhalation, *hevel*, vapor. *It* took from you what was rightfully yours. Can we master that *it* Abel? Of course we can, and we damn well should."

All of the stories Cain has recently heard are instantly drummed out of his head. Raising his arm with the stone still in hand, he yells, "*I* am the victim."

Aaron brings his face right up to Cain's face, looks at him with neither malice nor mercy, says to him right in his face, "Sin lied to you."

Cain remembers again, this time, the stern and trembling, all-powerful and impotent voice of God: "Abel is your brother. You don't have to love him; you don't have to like him. But he is your brother, and you are not his master. It's *Sin* crouching at the door who you can master, who you must try to master, not because you love Abel, not because you like Abel, but because you are *his* brother."

Disregarded for these moments by Cain, Sin coos at him even more enticingly: "Cain, you've been shamed. What are you waiting for? Take back your power. Cain, shame, Cain, shame . . ." God wants to hurl Sin into space, but God also knows that if God does, it will not matter. Sin will always be back to seduce Cain or some other person into snuffing out someone else's life.

Aaron, too, wonders if what he did, what he is doing, will matter when Sin is guaranteed to return.

He wonders whether it will matter if you and I, each of us, all of us, return to the killing field and place ourselves in the brothers' places, interpose our own struggles and lives, listen to their stories and our own, first and last, as brothers and sisters.

Yes, he thinks, *that will matter.*

He wonders whether it will matter if you and I, each of us, all of us, Noah's descendants, recognize ourselves as both Cain and Abel. Will it matter if we grasp that we have both the power and the obligation to choose those parts of ourselves that bring life and not death?

Yes, he thinks, *that will matter.*

Suddenly, Aaron breaks out of his reverie. He's being hurled back to Moses, the Israelites, God, the open desert expanse between slavery and freedom. He wonders, one last time, *will it matter?* . . . And this time he is comforted all the more. Not by an answer, exactly, but by a gift he and we, all of humanity, now have—the hope-filled, haunting and healing, eternally sustaining, waiting-to-be answered question:

Am I my brother's keeper?

Notes

Introduction

1. Springsteen, *Born to Run*, 406–14, 484–88.
2. Springsteen, *Born to Run*, 265.
3. Claudius, Hamlet's uncle who murdered Hamlet's father, says to himself: "O, my offense is rank, it smells to high heaven; it hath the primal eldest curse upon 't, a brother's murder." Shakespeare, *Hamlet*, Act 3, Scene 3, lines 39–41, 84.
4. Professor Timothy Lytton points out that the empaneled judges in mishnaic-era capital cases served a kind of hybrid function: as judges and jury of experts debating each case. See Kehati, *Mishnah Seder Nezikin*, vol. 2, *Sanhedrin* 4:5, 54–55. Based on private correspondence between the author and Professor Lytton.
5. Kehati, *Mishnah Seder Nezikin*, vol. 2, *Sanhedrin* 4:5, 54–55.
6. The only other remotely legal reference to Cain and Abel in Rabbinic literature that this author is aware of is a fanciful explanation for why Jews are forbidden from wearing clothing that contains a blend of linen and wool. See Leviticus 19:19 and Deuteronomy 25:11. Cain's insufficient offering to God seems to have been flax seeds, from which linen is derived. Abel offered the best of his flock, presumably sheep, the source of wool. Per this line of reasoning, Jews are forbidden from blending materials used by Cain, the murderer, with materials used by Abel, the victim. Fano, *Midrash Tanḥuma*, 17.
7. In actuality, Cain's mark served as a protective mark. God placed it on Cain to prevent others from killing him in exile.

8. For an early example of the concept, specifically referring to the power of meditative prayer, see Matt, *The Zohar*, vol. 6, II:216a, 229. See also Jacobson-Maisels, *"Tikkun Olam,"* 353–82.

9. Theodor and Albeck, *Bereschit Rabba*, 8:5, 60; Freedman and Simon, *Midrash Rabbah: Genesis*, 1:58.

10. Visotzky, *Reading the Book*, 183–203.

11. Quoted in Goldsmith and Scult, *Dynamic Judaism*, 104.

12. Specifically, Eve gave birth to three girls, one a twin of Cain's and two of them triplets with Abel. They became the wives of the brothers, who are said to have fought one another for sexual and reproductive control over them. Theodor and Albeck, *Bereschit Rabba*, 205; Freedman and Simon, *Midrash Rabbah: Genesis*, 1:180.

13. See *Mekhilta D'Rabbi Ishmael*, Parshat B'Shallah, Massekhta D'Shirah, 7.

1. Reading Cain and Abel

1. Marilynne Robinson, "Book of Books: What Literature Owes the Bible," *New York Times Sunday Book Review*, December 22, 2011, https://www .nytimes.com/2011/12/25/books/review/the-book-of-books-what -literature-owes-the-bible.html.

2. The next ten verses, Genesis 4:17–26, are an integral part of the Cain and Abel story cycle and an important postscript to the murder story, containing critical insights about Cain's life and lineage and the development of civilization in the aftermath of his crime.

3. This description of Sin in the Hebrew text can also be translated as, "At the entrance is sin, a crouching demon, toward you his lust—but you can rule over him," per Everett Fox's Torah translation. See Fox, *The Five Books of Moses*, 27.

4. JPS Hebrew-English TANAKH, 7–8.

5. Malbim to Gen. 4:1, Weisser, *Torah Im Perush Ha-Malbim*, 70–73.

6. Friedman, *Who Wrote The Bible?*, 15–32.

7. Wellhausen, *Prolegomena to the History of Ancient Israel*, 297–304.

2. Balancing Justice and Mercy

1. Ray, *Knock on Any Door*.

2. Bosley Crowther, "The Screen in Review: Humphrey Bogart, John Derek Seen in 'Knock on Any Door,' New Tenant at Astor," *New York Times*, February 23, 1949, 31.

3. Theodor and Albeck, *Bereschit Rabba* 12:15, 112–13; Freedman and Simon, *Midrash Rabbah: Genesis*, 1:99. See also Urbach, *The Sages*, 448–61.

4. David Stern, a renowned scholar of midrash, explains that these stories are not logically consistent analogies but creative ways of talking about God in relationship with people. Many *mashal* stories present God anthropomorphically as a king who has emotional highs and lows and who engages in paradoxical behavior that often seems irrational and even inexcusable. Why present God as a human ruler who is less than perfect and even prone to volatility? Professor Stern responds: "The rabbis were able to portray God's full complexity only by imagining Him in the human image. Why? Because only human behavior presented the rabbis with a model sufficiently complex to do justice to God." See Stern, *Parables in Midrash*, 101.

5. Professor Stern explained to this author that this *mashal* is not about testing the strength of the glasses; it is about praising God's ability to balance existence with equal measures of justice and mercy.

6. By the first century CE, Roman glass production was a highly accomplished and commercially successful industry across the empire. This was especially the case after the invention of glassblowing, which allowed for the creation of much finer, more delicate objects of high functional and artistic value. Double-handled glass cups, in particular, were in great demand in the Roman world of the Common Era. Thus, we might imagine the king being worried that his glass cups are so fine that they cannot survive actual use. See Trentinella, "Roman Glass."

7. Since glassmaking was an artisanal, "hands-on" industry in the Roman Empire, it is doubtful that Roman ruling families would have been involved in it. Nonetheless, according to Professor Rosemarie Trentinella, with whom this author engaged in private correspondence, a glass artisan could rise above this station and become part of the ruling class.

8. In ancient manuscripts that preserved this story, the other version of this word is *reikim,* "empty glasses." Here, the first version, *dakim,* delicate or fragile glasses, has been selected, because it emphasizes far more forcefully the fragile nature of creation, humanity, and God's choices. Interestingly, these two versions are based on the tiniest of changes that a scribe copying each version would have made to the Hebrew letter *resh,* ר, changing it into a *dalet,* ד.

3. Introducing Our Expert Witnesses

1. For more information on the use of expert witnesses in American courts, see Cornell Law School Legal Information Institute, "Federal Rules of Evidence."

2. Genesis 3:24 states explicitly that God drove Cain's parents, Eve and Adam, out of Eden.

3. Theodor and Albeck, *Bereschit Rabba* 22:16, 220; Freedman and Simon, *Midrash Rabbah: Genesis*, 1:191–92.

4. Two Talmuds exist, one edited by the Jews of Babylonia and the other edited by the Jews of the Land of Israel. Though students of Jewish law study both, the Babylonian Talmud became the authoritative source for deriving and codifying Jewish law and religious practice.

5. Babylonian Talmud, *Tractate Sanhedrin* 37b.

6. Babylonian Talmud, *Tractate Shabbat* 63a.

7. Porton, *Understanding Rabbinic Midrash*, 10–11.

8. If a Talmudic interpretation of a Torah law was the basis for established religious practice, the *parshanim* would generally accept that interpretation, even if they possessed an alternative explanation.

9. Chavel, *Peirushei Ha-torah Ramban*, 45; Chavel, *Nachmanides*, 92.

10. For instance, the modern critical Bible scholar E. A. Speiser explains that the name of Cain's final settlement, Nod (lit., "wandering"), is a symbol for Cain's retreat to a faraway place beyond Eden. He compares this with the story of Utnapishtim (the "Babylonian version of Noah"), who, according to the ancient Near Eastern Gilgamesh epic, retreated "faraway" after his flood ordeal had ended. Modern biblical scholarship often uses its knowledge of parallel cultures and literatures among the Israelites' neighbors to examine early influences on Israelite biblical writing. Ancient and medieval Rabbis would not have had access to these resources. See Speiser, *The Anchor Bible: Genesis*, 31.

11. For more about medieval Jewish Bible interpretation, see Harris, "Medieval Jewish Biblical Exegesis," 141–71; and Greenstein, "Medieval Bible Commentaries," 213–60.

4. Competent to Stand Trial?

1. My imaginary assessment is based on the forensic mental health assessment report used in the State of Florida circuit court. See Thirteenth Judicial Circuit of Florida, "Sample Evaluation Form."

2. Dr. Eliezer Finkelman points out eight possible ways the ancient Rabbis could have read this ambiguous phrase, including reading it as Cain's rhetorical questions to God as an attempt to blame his behavior on God. See Finkelman, "Cain's (Im)penitent Response to His Punishment."

3. See Cassuto, *Commentary on the Book of Genesis*, 212–13.

4. This is different from the noun *mashal*, a "proverb" or "parable."

5. The author's wife, Marian Alexander, notes that Eve and Adam would have had no models — except for animal families — on which to base their parenting decisions for their adult sons. In fact, since most other animal species do not interact with their adult young, why and how would Eve and Adam have known to raise their young differently?

6. In fact, God caused everything to grow by itself as a part of the initial creative process. See Genesis 1 and Genesis 2:15.

7. Finkelstein, *Sifre al Sefer Devarim*, 87; Hammer, *Sifrei: Deuteronomy*, 85.

8. Abraham Ibn Ezra (1089–1167) was a prominent biblical scholar, philosopher, and grammarian who lived during the "Golden Age" of medieval Spanish Jewry.

9. Krinsky, *Meḥóqeqé Yehudah*, 54. Ibn Ezra's simple explanation seems to consciously ignore the earlier references in the book of Genesis to the four rivers watering Eden as well as to Adam's naming of the animals, which would have given him control over them.

5. Interrogating the Interrogator

1. For some of the formulaic language in this imaginary deposition of God, see Ando, "Deposition Tips."

2. By mention of the date of Nisan 17, 0041, God is noted to be testifying at the deposition three days after Nisan 14, 0041, the date it is said that Cain murdered Abel. According to a Rabbinic legend, Adam looked into the future, then commanded his sons to make offerings to God on the fourteenth of the Hebrew month of Nisan, on what would later be the eve of the first Passover offering. Just as God would protect the Israelites from the Egyptian plague of the death of the firstborn through the sacrificial blood smeared on their doors, Cain and Abel could propitiate God through their own offerings. This rather unlikely but instructive scenario seems to set up a profound moral and literary irony in the Rabbis' reading of the Cain and Abel story. A religious act that should have brought the brothers together for the sake of perpetuating life precipi-

tated the first murder and the further decline of civilization. Bleier, *Sefer Pirke D'Rabbi Eliezer*, 178–79; Friedlander, *Pirke de Rabbi Eliezer*, 153.

3. YHVH, one of God's seven names found in the Bible, and the one used in the original Hebrew text of Genesis 4, derives from the Hebrew verb root *h-v-h*, "to be." Because the name was considered extremely sacred, and its original proper pronunciation was uncertain, it was revocalized in the early centuries of the Common Era. We pronounce YHVH as *Adonai*, "Lord."

4. Cain's response to God—in Hebrew, "*gadol avoni min'so*"—can also be translated, "My punishment is too great to bear."

5. Cassuto, *Commentary on the Book of Genesis*, 225.

6. Seven variations of the Hebrew word *aḥ*, "brother," are found in Genesis 4. Repetition of words for emphasis is a common technique in biblical literature.

7. Finkelman, "Cain's (Im)Penitent Response to His Punishment."

8. Theodor and Albeck, *Bereschit Rabba* 8:5, 60; Freedman and Simon, *Midrash Rabbah: Genesis*, 1:58. In this story, God literally tosses Truth to the earth, in keeping with the verse from Psalms 85:11–12, quoted by the storyteller, Rabbi Simon.

9. Later talmudic tradition picks up on God's parental compassion when it declares that from beginning to end, the Torah is all about compassion, divine and human. God clothes Eve and Adam at the beginning (Gen. 3) and personally buries Moses at the end (Deut. 34). See Babylonian Talmud, *Tractate Sotah* 14a.

6. Day One of the Trial

1. For a model of a criminal trial transcript, see California Courts, "Mock Trial Script."

2. Ornstein, "Cain and Maples." In the original published version of the poem, the pronoun "He" was used to refer to God. Here, it has been replaced with the word "God."

3. Conrad, *Three Short Novels*, 84.

4. Kehati, *Mishnayot Mevuarot: Sanhedrin*, 385; Kehati, *Mishnah*, 54–57.

5. Babylonian Talmud, *Tractate Sanhedrin* 37a.

6. Wiesel, *Messengers of God*, 60–61.

7. This is the Torah's etymology of Kayyin's name, though it is not necessarily the correct derivation in biblical Hebrew. In sister languages of

Hebrew such as Arabic and Aramaic, the word means "to fashion," "to shape," "to give form" to something. A secondary meaning of the word is a smith or metal worker who gives shape and form to raw material. Thus, Kayyin is a creature formed by Eve in conjunction with God. Cassuto, *Commentary on the Book of Genesis*, 196–202.

8. Genesis 25:27–34 and Deuteronomy 21:15–17.

9. Malbim on Genesis 4:1–2 makes the point that ancient people would consecrate their firstborn for sacred service while their younger children were assigned to lesser, more profane tasks. For Eve, Cain was of primary importance, and Abel was of secondary importance. Weisser, *Torah Im Perush Ha-Malbim*, 71.

10. Babylonian Talmud, *Tractate Megillah* 3a.

11. Targum Yonatan ben Uzziel on Genesis 4:1 in Samet and Bitton, *Mikraot Gedolot*, 95; Bleier, *Sefer Pirke D'Rabbi Eliezer*, 177; Friedlander, *Pirke Rabbi Eliezer*, 150–51. *Pirke D'Rabbi Eliezer* interprets the words "Adam knew Eve, his wife" to mean that he knew about her infidelity when he recognized Cain's resemblance to someone other than himself, a celestial being. Though it provides us with interesting speculation about Cain, Rabbi ben Uzziel's interpretation of Eve's declaration is not widely accepted; the more common interpretation is that Eve was exulting in her powers as a co-creator and rival with God. See Cassuto, *Commentary on the Book of Genesis*, 196–202, who translates our verse, "I have created a man equally with the Lord."

12. Rabbi ben Uzziel's story about angels and humans making children together is based on Genesis 6:1–4. Also, the Hebrew *et Adonai* can be rendered as "in partnership with a godlike being."

13. Chavel, *Peirushei Rashi al Ha-torah*, 20; Herczeg, *The Torah: With Rashi's Commentary*, 42.

14. Onkelos, commentary on Genesis 4:7, in Samet and Bitton, *Mikraot Gedolot*, 98–100.

15. Barmash, *Homicide in the Biblical World*, 12–13. See also Barmash's translation of the Cain and Abel story in the same source, as well as that of Everett Fox, in *Five Books of Moses*, 25–29.

16. Theodor and Albeck, *Bereschit Rabba*, 22:5, 213–15; Freedman and Simon, *Midrash Rabbah: Genesis*, 1:187. For an interesting take on the message of Cain and Abel, see Cohen, "Enochville," 75–84.

17. Targum Yonatan ben Uzziel on Genesis 4:8, in Samet and Bitton, *Mikraot Gedolot*, 100. For a more formal translation of Rabbi ben Uzziel's interpretation, see Wiesel, *Messengers of God*, 66–67.

18. However, we also need to bear in mind what Rabbi ben Uzziel does not say explicitly: the equally valid possibility that God's choice was entirely justified and morally just, the quality of Cain's offerings notwithstanding. A simple, contextual reading of the Torah reminds us of Abel's severe disadvantages. His mother seems to take no interest in him, and he is the younger son, thus more vulnerable economically and in terms of his family status. We should keep open the possibility that even if Cain's offering had been the best on the planet, God would nonetheless privilege Abel to give him a fighting chance of survival against those vulnerabilities. This is suggested in God's deposition.

19. Werblowsky and Wigoder, *Oxford Dictionary of the Jewish Religion*, 673; Babylonian Talmud, *Tractate Sanhedrin* 39a.

20. The Hebrew term for "keeper," *shomer*, has a very specific legal connotation in the Torah and later Rabbinic writings: a bailee, or someone who is legally responsible for property that the owner has given him for safekeeping, either on a voluntary or a paid basis. Though the Cain and Abel story is a nonlegal narrative, it uses legal ideas of the Torah to make its larger moral and spiritual arguments. Here, ironically, Cain is condemning himself by refusing to acknowledge that his blood kin is given to him by God, his "Owner," for the sacred task of mutual safekeeping. Barmash, *Homicide in the Biblical World*, 18.

21. While the Mishnah's interpretation of "your brother's blood" in Hebrew is literally "bloods," *damim*, this Hebrew word is also a legal term for blood guilt: culpability imposed on a murderer for having spilled blood, not only by having taken a life but also by having polluted the earth and the community. Pamela Barmash explains the twofold nature of blood in biblical thinking: It can purify the community of sin through specific animal offerings, and it can also pollute the earth when it is spilled during murder. Thus, as she elucidates, Abel is silenced by Cain, but his blood cries out of the earth where it was spilled, seeking justice and the restoration of communal balance and healing after the crime. Barmash, *Homicide in the Biblical World*, 14, 17–18.

22. Fano, *Midrash Tanḥuma*, 18.

23. Finkelman, "Cain's (Im)Penitent Response to His Punishment."

7. Day Two of the Trial

1. A passage in the Babylonian Talmud, *Tractate Yoma* 52a–b, declares this verse to be one of five passages in the Torah whose ambiguous syntax does not allow us to determine its true meaning. One aspect of this ambiguity hinges on the Hebrew word *se'et*, from the verb root *n-s-a*, "to bear aloft" or "to carry." In this biblical verse, *se'et* could mean "you will be uplifted," meaning that by doing well, Cain would be lifted up morally, as well as lifted up from his depression and his loss to Abel. It could also mean "you will bear or carry your sinful behavior." Placed exactly in the center of the verse, *se'et* can be read as the end of the first clause in the verse or as the beginning of the second clause: "If you, Cain, do well, you will be uplifted" or "You will bear the consequences of your bad behavior if you do not do well." However, the verse does not need to be interpreted ambiguously. It can be read as God's warning to Cain about his physical and emotional low places in which Sin awaits him.

2. In the Babylonian Talmud, *Tractate Sotah* 3a teaches that the only time a person sins is when he or she gets "possessed" by a spirit of stupidity. Later commentators explain that sin is the antithesis of reason and common sense.

3. Novelist John Steinbeck's master work *East of Eden* deals with these exact approaches to translating *ve-attah timshol bo*. Steinbeck, *East of Eden*, 299–302.

4. Satan is the Hebrew word for God's heavenly accuser angel who attempts to incite God's anger against people by calling their righteousness into question. Christian biblical literature and early Church teachings more fully developed Satan into a fallen angel, a semi-independent figure who challenges God's power and dominion and seduces individuals into sin through possession of their souls. However, it should be noted that Christian Bible stories of God's apocalyptic battles with Satan share roots with ancient Jewish and Near Eastern apocalypse legends as well as stories about God's battles with primordial monsters of chaos. See Psalms 74:12–16; Job 1–2; and Daniel 7. Also see Levine and Brettler, *Jewish Annotated New Testament*, 482–83.

5. Ginzberg, *Legends of the Bible*, 34–35. Lilith, the first wife of Adam alluded to in Genesis 1, leaves him because he refuses to treat her as his equal. She is transformed into a night demon who, according to Jewish

legend, tries to destroy newborns in their cribs. *Legends* is a one-volume version of Professor Ginzberg's classic seven-volume work, *Legends of the Jews* (1909), also published by The Jewish Publication Society.

6. Akkad was a late third-millennium BCE empire in what is present-day Iraq. Its literary and religious culture produced important works that influenced biblical stories, especially the creation and Noah narratives.

7. Barmash, *Homicide in the Biblical World*, 5–16.

8. The Bible considered the heart to be the seat of emotions and impulses. See, for instance, Genesis 6:5 and 8:21, which acknowledge that the devisings of the human heart are persistently evil.

9. Barmash, *Homicide in the Biblical World*, 14–16; Cassuto, *Commentary on the Book of Genesis*, 208–13; Speiser, *The Anchor Bible: Genesis*, 32–33.

10. See Genesis 1:27. Equally problematic is the Torah's seeming characterization of Sin as a temptress. This reflects a common misogynistic stereotype of women as seductresses who lead good men to do evil.

11. Genesis 4:7. Brettler and Berlin, *Jewish Study Bible*, 200–204. Hata'at, Hebrew for "sin," is also an ambiguous word. It can mean sin as well as purification from sin, as seen in the hata'at offering mentioned numerous times in the book of Leviticus, for instance, Leviticus 4.

12. The image of Sin as a femme fatale or man-eater demonizes women as the embodiment of sinful temptation seeking to destroy men. It also presents men as the exclusive actors in moral decision making, as they fight the demonic wiles of female temptation.

13. Cassuto, *Commentary on the Book of Genesis*, 208–13.

14. The early Rabbis already anticipated a similar meaning in this grammatical problem, howbeit in a way that once again stereotypes women. They used it to show how when Sin first enters a person, it is as "weak as a woman." Ultimately, Sin "overcomes a person with the power of a man," as we succumb to our impulses. Theodor and Albeck, *Bereschit Rabba*, 210; Freedman and Simon, *Midrash Rabbah: Genesis*, 1:185.

15. The phrase originated in the biblical story of Noah's ark and the Great Flood (Gen. 6–9). The Flood was the devastating result of God's bitter regret at how humanity had turned out many generations after Cain and his family had lived. Twice in the Noah narrative, the Torah acknowledges that the nature (*yetzer*) or devisings of the human heart are persistently evil.

16. A far more positive Rabbinic view of *yetzer ha-ra* characterizes it as the psychic energy (what we might call libido) that, when channeled properly, motivates us to have sex and procreate, engage in business, follow our ambitions, and build society. Schechter, *Some Aspects of Rabbinic Theology*, 219–92.

17. Babylonian Talmud, *Tractate Kiddushin* 30b. Each biblical source that the talmudic story quotes ("as it is written") is taken directly from the Cain and Abel story, Genesis 4:7. The Talmud is using God's words from Genesis 4 to make a point about human beings' ability to conquer *yetzer ha-ra*. An interesting midrashic device is being employed here: God quotes the Torah's story to teach a new, related lesson.

18. David Stern identifies the complaint *mashal* as one type of *mashal* theme. The storyteller, speaking on behalf of the Jewish people, presents a parable in which a king's subjects complain about the king's unfairness. This is an apt rhetorical tool for launching into an impassioned protest against God for the subjection of God's subjects, the Jewish people, to suffering. While our *mashal* story lacks the explicit features of a complaint or protest *mashal*, it certainly hints at complaint and protest. Stern, *Parables in Midrash*, 30–134.

19. According to Christianity, original sin is a spiritual stain inherited by all human beings from Eve and Adam. Its destructive effects on our souls cannot be wiped away without belief in Jesus as a person's savior. How good we are is immaterial.

20. Kass, *Beginning of Wisdom*, 127–28.

21. As Stern explains, the initial function of *mashal* stories is exegetical — that is, they start out as a way to interpret the meaning and enduring relevance of biblical verses. Levine and Brettler, *Jewish Annotated New Testament*, 568; Stern, *Parables in Midrash*, 4–42.

22. According to Rabbinic teaching, *yetzer ha-tov* is an admonishing voice of conscience that cites biblical behavioral prohibitions in order to internally stir a person's good judgment and guilt when he or she reaches majority age: twelve for women and thirteen for men. Goldin, *Fathers According to Rabbi Nathan*, 83–84.

23. Kass, *Beginning of Wisdom*, 448.

8. Day Three of the Trial

1. See chapter 6, note 7, for the etymology of Cain's name.

2. The forensic assessment, presented in a table in chapter 4, demonstrates how the language of Genesis 4 echoes that of Genesis 3. Specifically, God tells Eve that her desire will be for Adam but that he will rule over her. When warning Cain later on about Sin, God tells him that Sin's desire will be directed at him but that he can rule over Sin. The Prosecution implies that Cain knew that the struggle to exercise self-restraint in the face of temptation was a long-standing challenge in his family to which he should have been attuned.

3. Pagis, *Points of Departure*, 22.

4. Until May 14, 1948, when Israel became a state, that area of the Middle East was governed by the British Empire's colonial mandate, which referred to it as Palestine, its name since the time of Roman imperial rule in the second century CE.

5. Lerner, *Eternally Eve*, 146.

6. Ginzberg, *Legends of the Bible*, 33–51.

7. The Rabbinic midrash about Eve's affair with Samael is admittedly a very troubling portrayal of her. It is one story in a series of early, rather misogynistic Eve legends. As noted in chapter 6, the present author has reappropriated the story to provide a nuanced portrayal of Eve as humanity's mother seeking to wrest life from death. Similar to her consuming the fruit of the Tree of Knowledge, her affair with Samael is a transgression against God, not to mention a betrayal of Adam. Paradoxically, this affair makes her pregnant with Cain, thus preserving human life outside of paradise and fulfilling God's earlier charge to the first humans to reproduce. It is Eve, not Adam, who will have the last word when she (with Adam's help, of course) gives birth to their third son, Seth, the progenitor of humanity through the line of Noah and his family after the Great Flood. She is the one who will declare that Seth represents new life and hope after their other children's fatal encounter: "God has provided me with another offspring in place of Abel" (Gen. 4:25).

8. Chavel, *Peirushei Ramban*, 45; Chavel, *Nachmanides*, 92.

9. This is an echo of God's curse on Adam. See Genesis 3:17–19.

10. Theodor and Albeck, *Bereschit Rabba*, 21:1, 198–201; Freedman and Simon, *Midrash Rabbah: Genesis*, 1:172–76.

11. Truth's assessment is plausible, but it is also bloodless. It leaves no room for us to confront the anguish of two traumatized and bereaved parents, one of

whom would do anything to protect her child, the fratricidal murderer. Following a more emotional line of interpretation, the poet Dan Pagis explains that Cain's crime was directed not only at his brother but their whole family. As he was silencing Abel, he was also silencing their parents, until finally Eve cried out against Cain's crimes . . . yet too late and to no avail.

Another explanation: Perhaps trauma—a blunt force trauma of one's heart—accounts for Eve and Adam's absence before, during, and right after Cain's fatal attack on his brother. No matter their imperfections and ambivalent feelings as parents, they loved their children. They watched helplessly as Cain's relationship with Abel deteriorated and culminated in this despicable act. God did not mention them in the crime report not because they were physically or even emotionally absent; they were just too stunned, too paralyzed, to speak.

9. Day Four of the Trial

1. This phrase is taken from the Bruce Springsteen song by the same title. Springsteen, "The Nothing Man," in *The Rising*.
2. According to midrashic sources, three biblical figures were so obsessed with agriculture, it ultimately destroyed them. Cain, Noah, and King Uzziah could think of doing nothing else, and thus abandoned studying Torah and serving God. Theodor and Albeck, *Bereschit Rabba* 22:3, 206; Freedman and Simon, *Midrash Rabbah: Genesis*, 1:181.
3. Theodor and Albeck, *Bereschit Rabba* 22:2, 205; Freedman and Simon, *Midrash Rabbah: Genesis*, 1:180.
4. According to midrashic sources, Abel's dog stood guard over his lifeless body to protect it from other animals. See Bleier, *Sefer Pirke D'Rabbi Eliezer*, 183.
5. Fano, *Midrash Tanḥuma*, 18.
6. Theodor and Albeck, *Bereschit Rabba* 22:9, 216; Freedman and Simon, *Midrash Rabbah: Genesis*, 1:189.
7. Abel's question echoes Abraham's challenge to God before God destroys the evil cities of Sodom and Gomorrah. See Genesis 18:25.

10. Day Four Continues

1. Steinbeck, *East of Eden*, 299–302.
2. Steinbeck actually mispronounced the word as *timshel*, for reasons that remain unexplained. There is also a fourth way of understanding

timshol, one that is admittedly pure conjecture but intriguing. The full Hebrew phrase spoken by God is *ve-attah timshol bo*, written in Hebrew as ואתה תמשול בו, "You may rule over sin." The letters could be rewritten in the following way as a question: ואת התמשול בו, "*V'aht, ha-timshol bo?*," "Will you, Cain, rule over Sin?" When we reattach the ending letter, *hei*, to the next word, *timshol*, it becomes an interrogative, a prefix denoting a question. Another complicating factor concerns the Hebrew female pronoun for "you," *aht*. There are a few instances in the TANAKH in which it serves as an address to a male. There are also a few instances of the Hebrew male pronoun for "*you*" (*attah*) being spelled as *aht*, though vocalized as *attah*. Read this way, the verse makes God's assurance of Cain's freedom to choose even more open ended and contingent than Steinbeck and others before him have construed it.

3. Malbim to Genesis 4:9, Weisser, *Torah Im Perush Ha-Malbim*, 73.

4. Spilling the murderer's blood would purify the earth that had been polluted by the victim's blood. Barmash, *Homicide in the Biblical World*, 14, 17–18.

5. This is based on a sample sentencing order from the Florida state court system. See National Judicial College, "Sample Sentencing Orders."

6. Theodor and Albeck, *Bereschit Rabba*, 22:12, 219; Freedman and Simon, *Midrash Rabbah: Genesis*, 1:191.

11. Beyond Cain

1. Theodor and Albeck, *Bereschit Rabba*, 22:13, 220; Freedman and Simon, *Midrash Rabbah: Genesis*, 1:192; Margoliot, *Midrash Ha-Gadol*, 120–21.

2. This midrashic rendering uses Lamech's strange speech to his wives as the interpretive basis for the equally strange story about the end of Cain and his line. For the reader's ease, the present author left out the earlier midrashic Sages' detailed interpretations of each verse of Lamech's speech to Ada and Zillah.

3. Fano, *Midrash Tanḥuma*, 19–20; Theodor and Albeck, *Bereschit Rabba*, 23:4, 224–26; Freedman and Simon, *Midrash Rabbah: Genesis*, 1:195.

4. Tubal-cain has a sister, Naamah, as well as two half-brothers, Adah's sons, Jabal and Jubal. Thus, Lamech accidentally kills one quarter of his descendants when he kills Tubal-cain. It is interesting that he kills Tubal-cain on the same day that he kills Cain. The death of Cain the murderer comes full circle with the death of his name.

5. Heschel, *Moral Grandeur and Spiritual Audacity*, 209. Rabbi Heschel, the celebrated theologian, activist, and writer, wrote these words as the Nazis were incinerating European Jewry as well as murdering millions of other human beings. A refugee from Nazi Europe who lost his entire family in the Holocaust, Heschel was a personal witness to "the mark of Cain" reflected in human behavior. He understood intimately human depravity, but this only made him more determined to hear God's demand that we be our brothers' keepers. He is as well known for his passionate political activism as for his writing.

Epilogue

1. *Mishnah Avot* 1:12.
2. Goldin, *Fathers According to Rabbi Nathan*, 63–65.
3. Dobyns, "Long Story," in *Velocities*, 249.

Bibliography

Ando, Russell. "Deposition Tips: What Is a Deposition?" *Caught.net and the Pro Se Way.* caught.net/prose/depositiontips/htm.

Babylonian Talmud. *Tractate Megillah. Tractate Sotah. Tractate Taanit. Tractate Yoma. Tractate Sanhedrin.* New York: Artscroll Series, Mesorah Publications, 1990.

Barmash, Pamela. *Homicide in the Biblical World.* Cambridge: Cambridge University Press, 2005.

Bleier, Yonatan, ed. *Sefer Pirke D'Rabbi Eliezer.* Jerusalem: Ohel Rabbeinu Yonoson Ublima Foundation, 2005.

Brettler, Marc, and Adele Berlin, eds. *The Jewish Study Bible.* New York: Oxford University Press, 2014.

Brown, Raymond, Joseph Fitzmyer, and Roland Murphy, eds. *The Jerome Biblical Commentary.* Englewood Cliffs NJ: Prentice Hall, 1968.

California Courts, the Judicial Branch of California. "Mock Trial Script: The Case of a Stolen Car." www.courts.ca.gov/documents/mocktrialscript -contra.pdf.

Cassuto, Umberto. *A Commentary on the Book of Genesis.* Part 1, *From Adam to Noah.* Translated by Israel Abrahams. Jerusalem: Magnes Press of the Hebrew University, 1972.

Chavel, Charles, trans. and ed. *Nachmanides, Commentary on the Torah: Genesis.* New York: Shilo Publishing House, 1971.

———, ed. *Peirushei Rashi al Ha-torah.* 4th ed. Jerusalem: Mossad Ha-Rav Kook, 1986.

———, ed. *Peirushei Ha-torah L'Rabbeinu Moshe ben Naḥman (Ramban)*. Vol. 1. Jerusalem: Mossad Ha-Rav Kook, 1982.

Coates, Ta-Nehisi. *Between the World and Me*. New York: Speigel & Grau, 2015.

Cohen, Martin. "Enochville." *Conservative Judaism* 53, no. 2 (Winter 2001): 75–84.

Cohen, Norman J. *Self, Struggle and Change: Family Conflict Stories in Genesis and Their Healing Insights for Our Lives*. Woodstock VT: Jewish Lights Publishing, 1995.

Conrad, Joseph. *Three Short Novels: Heart of Darkness, Youth, Typhoon*. New York: Bantam Books, 1960.

Cornell Law School Legal Information Institute. "Federal Rules of Evidence: Article VII. Opinions and Expert Testimony, Rule 702: Testimony by Expert Witness." https://www.law.cornell.edu/rules/fre/rule_702.

Cover, Robert. "Violence and the Word." In *Narrative, Violence, and the Law: The Essays of Robert Cover*, edited by Martha Minow, Michael Ryan, and Austin Sarat, 203–38. Ann Arbor: University of Michigan Press, 1993.

Diamond, Jared. *Guns, Germs, and Steel: The Fates of Human Societies*. New York: W.W. Norton, 2005.

———. *The Third Chimpanzee: The Evolution and Future of the Human Animal*. New York: HarperCollins, 2006.

Dobyns, Stephen. *Velocities: New and Selected Poems 1966–1992*. New York: Viking Penguin Books, 1994.

Fano, Ezra, ed. *Midrash Tanḥuma*. Jerusalem: Eshkol Books, 1972.

Finkelman, Eliezer. "Cain's Im(penitent) Response to His Punishment." *TheTorah.com*. http://thetorah.com/cains-im-penitent-response-to-his-punishment.

Finkelstein, Louis, ed. *Sifre al Sefer Devarim*. 2nd ed. New York: Jewish Theological Seminary of America, 1969.

Fox, Everett. *The Five Books of Moses: A New Translation with Introductions, Commentary and Notes*. New York: Schocken Books, 1995.

Freedman, Harry, and Maurice Simon, trans. and eds. *Midrash Rabbah: Genesis*. Vol. 1. New York: Soncino Press, 1983.

Friedlander, Gerald, ed. and trans. *Pirke de Rabbi Eliezer (The Chapters of Rabbi Eliezer the Great)*. New York: Hermon Press, 1970.

Friedman, Richard Elliott. *Who Wrote the Bible?* New York: Harper & Row, 1987.

Ginzberg, Louis. *Legends of the Bible*. Philadelphia: Jewish Publication Society, 1992.

Goldin, Judah, ed. and trans. *The Fathers According to Rabbi Nathan*. New Haven CT: Yale University Press, 1983.

Goldsmith, Emanuel S., and Mel Scult, eds. *Dynamic Judaism: The Essential Writings of Mordecai M. Kaplan*. New York: Fordham University Press/ Reconstructionist Press, 1985.

Greenstein, Edward L. "Medieval Bible Commentaries." In *Back to the Sources: Reading the Classic Jewish Texts*, edited by Barry Holtz, 213–60. New York and Philadelphia: Summit Books and Jewish Publication Society, 1984.

Hammer, Reuven, trans. *Sifrei: A Tannaitic Commentary on the Book of Deuteronomy*. New Haven CT: Yale University Press, 1986.

Harris, Robert A. "Medieval Jewish Biblical Exegesis." In *A History of Biblical Interpretation*, vol. 2, edited by Duane and Alan Watson, 141–71. Grand Rapids MI: Eerdman's Publishing, 2009.

Herczeg, Yisrael Isser Zvi. *The Torah: With Rashi's Commentary Translated, Annotated, and Elucidated: Genesis*. Brooklyn NY: Mesorah Publications, 2009.

Heschel, Abraham Joshua. *Moral Grandeur and Spiritual Audacity*. Edited by Susannah Heschel. New York: Farrar, Straus & Giroux, 1996.

———. *God in Search of Man: A Philosophy of Judaism*. New York: Farrar, Straus & Cudahy, 1955.

Hobbes, Thomas. *Of Man, Being the First Part of Leviathan*. Vol. 34, Pt. 5, of *The Harvard Classics*. New York: P.F. Collier & Son, 1909–14.

Jacobson-Maisels, James. "*Tikkun Olam, Tikkun Atzmi*: Healing the Self, Healing the World." In *Tikkun Olam*, edited by David Birnbaum and Martin Cohen, 353–82. New York: New Paradigm Matrix, 2014.

Jacoby, Russell. *Bloodlust: On the Roots of Violence from Cain and Abel to the Present*. New York: Free Press, 1999.

Jones, Daniel, ed. *The Poems of Dylan Thomas*. New York: New Directions Publishing, 1971.

JPS Hebrew-English TANAKH. Philadelphia: Jewish Publication Society, 1999.

Kass, Leon. *The Beginning of Wisdom: Reading Genesis*. Chicago: University of Chicago Press, 2006.

Katzenellenbogen, Mordechai, ed. *Torah Ḥayyim*. Vol. 1, *Breisheet*. Jerusalem: Mossad Ha-Rav Kook, 1993.

Kehati, Pinchas, ed. *The Mishnah: Seder Nezikin*. Vol. 2, *Bava Batra, Sanhedrin*. Translated by Rabbi Shmuel Himelstein. Jerusalem: Eliner Library Department for Torah Education and Culture in the Diaspora, 1994.

Krinsky, Yehudah Leib, ed. *Meḥóqeqé Yehudah al Perush Rabbi Avraham ibn Ezra La-torah.* Minsk, Russia: n.p., 1907.

Laughton, Charles, dir. *The Night of the Hunter.* United Artists, 1955.

Lee, Spike, dir. *Do the Right Thing.* Universal Pictures, 1989.

Lerner, Anne. *Eternally Eve: Images of Eve in the Bible, Midrash, and Modern Jewish Poetry.* Waltham MA: Brandeis University Press, 2007.

Levine, Amy-Jill, and Marc Brettler, eds. *The Jewish Annotated New Testament.* New York: Oxford University Press, 2011.

Margoliot, Mordechai, ed. *Midrash Ha-Gadol al Sefer Breisheet.* Jerusalem: Mossad Ha-Rav Kook, 1967.

———, ed. *Entziklopedia L'Toledot G'dolei Yisrael.* Vols. 1–4. Tel Aviv: Y. Orenstein and Yavneh Publishing, 1992.

———, ed. *Entziklopedia L'Ḥachmei Ha-Talmud.* Vols. 1–2. Tel Aviv: Y. Orenstein and Yavneh Publishing House, 1981.

Matt, Daniel, trans. and ed. *The Zohar: Pritzker Edition.* Vol. 6. Stanford CA: Stanford University Press, 2011.

Mekhilta de-Rabbi Ishmael. Translated by Jacob Z. Lauterbach. Philadelphia: Jewish Publication Society, 2004.

National Judicial College. "Sample Sentencing Orders." https://www.judges .org/capitalcasesresources/bookpdf/appendices/Sample%20Sentencing %20Orders.pdf.

Ornstein, Dan. "Cain and Maples: The Villain's Villanelle." *Jewish Literary Journal,* December 2014. http://jewishliteraryjournal.com/poetry/cain -and-maples/.

———. "Eden's Travelers: A Jewish Encounter with Humility, Ambition and Arrogance." In *Search for Meaning,* edited by David Birnbaum and Martin Cohen, 153–74. New York: New Paradigm Matrix, 2018.

Pagis, Dan. *Points of Departure.* Translated by Stephen Mitchell. Philadelphia: Jewish Publication Society, 1981.

Porton, Gary. *Understanding Rabbinic Midrash: Texts and Commentary.* Hoboken NJ: Ktav Publishing, 1985.

Power, Samantha. *A Problem from Hell: America and the Age of Genocide.* New York: Basic Books, 2013.

Ray, Nicholas, dir. *Knock on Any Door.* Columbia Pictures, 1949.

Sacks, Jonathan. *Not in God's Name: Confronting Religious Violence.* New York: Schocken Books, 2015.

Samet, Aharon, and Daniel Bitton. *Mikraot Gedolot: Ha-Maor Edition*. Jerusalem: Ha-Maor Institute, 1990.

Sarna, Nahum, ed. *The JPS Torah Commentary: Genesis*. Philadelphia: Jewish Publication Society, 1991.

Schechter, Solomon. *Some Aspects of Rabbinic Theology*. New York: Macmillan, 1909.

————, ed. *Massechet Avot D'Rabbi Natan*. Vienna: Ch. D. Lippe, 1887.

Shakespeare. *Hamlet*. Edited by Louis B. Wright and Virginia A. Lamar. The Folger Library General Reader's Shakespeare. New York: Pocket Books/ Simon and Schuster, 1959.

Skolnik, Fred, and Michael Berenbaum, eds. *Encyclopedia Judaica*. 2nd ed. Vols. 1–22. Jerusalem: Keter Publishing, 2007.

Speiser, E. A., trans. and ed. *The Anchor Bible: Genesis*. New York: Doubleday, 1964.

Springsteen, Bruce. *Darkness on the Edge of Town*. Columbia Records, 1978.

————. *The Rising*. Columbia Records, 2002.

————. *Born to Run*. New York: Simon & Schuster, 2016.

Steinbeck, John. *East of Eden*. New York: Penguin Books, 2002.

Stern, David. *Parables in Midrash: Narrative and Exegesis in Rabbinic Literature*. Cambridge MA: Harvard University Press, 1991.

Theodor, Jehudah, and Chanoch Albeck, eds. *Bereschit Rabba (Midrash Genesis Rabbah)*. Berlin: Akademie Verlag, 1929.

Thirteenth Judicial Circuit of Florida. "Sample Evaluation Form: Forensic Mental Health Assessment Report to the Circuit Court Chapter 916, Part II, Florida Statutes." http://www.fljud13.org/Portals/0/Forms/pdfs /SampleEvalualtionForm.pdf.

Trentinella, Rosemarie. "Roman Glass." *Heilbrunn Timeline of Art History*. New York: Metropolitan Museum of Art, October 2003. https://www .metmuseum.org/toah/hd/rgls/hd_rgls.htm.

Urbach, Ephraim. *The Sages: Their Concepts and Beliefs*. Translated by Israel Abrahams. Jerusalem: Magnes Press of Hebrew University, 1979.

Visotzky, Burton L. *Reading the Book: Making the Bible a Timeless Text*. New York: Anchor Books, 1991.

Weisser, Meir Leibush ben Yehiel Mikhel (Malbim). *Torah Im Perush Ha-Malbim: Sefer Breisheet*. B'nei Berak, Israel: Privately published, n.d.

Wellhausen, Julius. *Prolegomena to the History of Israel*. Translated by J. Sutherland Black and Allan Menzies. Edinburgh: Charles and Adam Black, 1885.

Werblowsky, R. J. Zwi, and Geoffrey Wigoder, eds. *The Oxford Dictionary of the Jewish Religion*. New York: Oxford University Press, 1997.

Wiesel, Elie. *Messengers of God: Biblical Portraits and Legends*. New York: Touchstone-Simon and Schuster, 1976.

Discussion and Activity Guide

Syllabus

I. Wrestling with the Text Questions
1. Cain and God (chapters 5 and 10)
2. Cain Himself (chapter 6)
3. Cain and Sin (chapter 7)
4. Cain and His Parents (chapters 4 and 8)
5. Cain and Abel (chapter 9)
6. Cain, Crime, and Consequences (chapters 6, 7, and 10)
7. Beyond Cain: Aftermath of the Trial (chapter 11)

II. Activities
1. Do a staged or informal reading of one or more of the courtroom transcripts.
2. Write and/or perform a suggested midrashic "what if?" skit.
3. Create a rap song or poem from a scenario with a twist.
4. Assign roles (e.g., political scientist, criminologist, feminist scholar) and have a roundtable discussion of their suggested questions.
5. Illustrate one of these scenes.

I. Wrestling with the Text Questions

The following questions, organized largely by chapters in this volume, can facilitate discussion in study groups, classes, and general conversations.

1. CAIN AND GOD

(chapters 5 and 10)

☐ Given the relationship between Cain's parents and God (Gen. 2–3), what might Cain have believed about God before Cain offered his gift to God?

☐ What do you think God is telling Cain when God says, "If you do right there is uplift"? (Gen. 4:7)

☐ Do you believe God's warning to Cain was ambiguous? If so, why would God give Cain an ambiguous warning?

☐ Since Cain had no prior experience with murder and its consequences, should he be expected to know what sinful impulses and behavior are?

☐ Was God's warning sufficient for Cain to be held responsible for his behavior?

☐ Had God not warned Cain at all, should Cain still be held responsible for his behavior?

☐ The Hebrew for Cain's words, *gadol avoni min'so*, can mean "my sin is too great to bear" or "my punishment is too great to bear." Given God's confrontation with Cain after the murder, is Cain showing God his capacity to ask for forgiveness or is he complaining to God about the severity of God's punishment?

☐ Based on your reading of the whole story, after God confronts Cain, does Cain grow emotionally and morally?

2. CAIN HIMSELF

(chapter 6)

☐ Before committing murder, is Cain depressed, enraged, or both? How else might you characterize his state of mind?

□ What role do familial relationships play in Cain's mind-set and crime?

□ Might God's warning have affected Cain's state of mind before he committed murder?

□ Must we the jury take Cain's state of mind into account in determining his responsibility for what he has done?

□ To what extent should Cain's relationships with family, God, and himself be mitigating factors in assessing his responsibility for killing Abel?

□ Was Cain's act of murder premeditated or not? Was it cold and calculating or hot and passionate? Could it be both simultaneously? Should the question of premeditation figure into Cain's sentence?

□ Just before the murder, Cain says something undisclosed to Abel, then kills him. What do you believe Cain says to his brother?

□ Most commentators take Cain's question, "Am I my brother's keeper?" to be a cynical rhetorical statement. However, at least one commentator we read, the Malbim, asserts that Cain genuinely did not understand that he was responsible for Abel. Which point of view is closest to your own? How does your viewpoint on this question influence your interpretation of the story?

3. CAIN AND SIN

(chapter 7)

□ Who or what is Sin?

□ Is Sin an outside force that enters us through environmental influences or the behavioral outcome of our inborn impulses and moral freedom?

□ God mentions Sin's presence to Cain in a way that leads us to infer that Cain already knows who or what Sin is. Has Cain already experienced the power of Sin or has he learned about Sin from his parents?

□ Why is Sin couching or crouching at the door? What door?

- ☐ If Sin is such a potent force of destruction, to what extent should Cain be held responsible for his actions?
- ☐ In speaking with Cain, God seems to connect Cain's depression and rage with Sin's ominous presence. Is the Bible implying that depression, rage, and envy are sinful, that they make us vulnerable to sinful behavior, or that they are the emotional aftermaths of sinful behavior?
- ☐ God tells Cain that Cain has the free will and capacity to master Sin. How can Cain do this?
- ☐ Why doesn't God ever spell out for Cain how to exercise self-control?
- ☐ The talmudic passage about the king who wounded his son found in the commentary in chapter 7 compares God's creation of people with sinful impulses to a parent who inflicts a severe, unhealed wound upon his or her child. What do you think of this analogy? What might such a story say about God?

4. CAIN AND HIS PARENTS

(chapters 4 and 8)

- ☐ After naming Cain, Eve disappears from the biblical story until after Cain's sentencing. The story never mentions Adam's presence, except to indicate that he is Cain's biological father. Why do you believe Eve and Adam are present only at the beginning and ending of this story?
- ☐ Though it is highly speculative, even far-fetched, the suggestion that Adam was not Cain's biological father plays an outsized role in this book. Is knowing Cain's family history necessary or irrelevant to understanding why he murdered Abel?
- ☐ Is knowing Cain's family history necessary or irrelevant in deciding Cain's sentence?
- ☐ What responsibility might Eve and Adam have played in the brothers' conflict and in Cain's psyche?
- ☐ How might parental favoritism have affected the brothers' relationships with God?

☐ Eve explains the meaning of Cain's name when he is born, but never explains Abel's name. Why?

☐ In chapter 4, Truth draws close language parallels between Genesis 3 (Eve and Adam's expulsion from Eden) and Genesis 4 (Cain and Abel). Do you believe Cain and Abel's experiences echo their parents' experiences?

☐ In his song "Adam Raised a Cain," Bruce Springsteen comments that we pay "for the sins of somebody else's past," in our case, as inheritors of Cain's violence toward Abel. What is your opinion of this idea?

5. CAIN AND ABEL

(chapter 9)

☐ What factors precipitated and fueled the brothers' sibling rivalry?

☐ Was the rivalry two-sided, or was it coming solely from Cain?

☐ Some Bible scholars have speculated that Cain the farmer and Abel the shepherd embody the historic conflict between agriculturalists and hunter-gatherers in early human history. What do you think of this interpretation? More generally, do such interpretations distort the main message of the story or help the reader to better understand it as a response to real-world human events?

☐ What might the brothers' respective offerings to God tell us about how each of them understood his relationship with God?

☐ Might God bear some responsibility for the brothers' individual choice of offerings? Does it matter?

☐ God never explains to Cain God's reason for accepting Abel's offering over his. Why do you believe God heeded Abel and his offering but not Cain's?

☐ Is God's decision justified? Does it matter?

☐ The biblical text provides us with no texture for Abel. He provides God with an offering, but otherwise he does not speak or do anything. Why do you think Abel is given no voice or substance in the text?

6. CAIN, CRIME, AND CONSEQUENCES

(chapters 6, 7, and 10)

☐ Abel is never heard from prior to the murder, yet God tells Cain that Abel's spilled blood cries out from the ground. What does God mean by this?

☐ Why do you believe God queries Cain, "Where is your brother?" Does God truly not know what Cain has done, is God giving Cain a chance to repent, or is God testing Cain's ability to take responsibility for his actions?

☐ What might Cain's response, "Am I my brother's keeper?," tell us about Cain's state of mind following the murder?

☐ Should Cain's state of mind after the murder factor into determining his punishment? If so, to what extent?

☐ Why do you believe God never answers Cain's response, "Am I my brother's keeper?"?

☐ How do you understand God's question to Cain, "What have you done?"? What is God trying to get from Cain? Is God's question an effective strategy in achieving it?

☐ What do you believe the full exchange (including its silences) is meant to teach us?

☐ Why do you believe God sentences Cain to a form of protected exile in which God marks him as off-limits to would-be avengers of Abel's blood? Why doesn't God sentence Cain to death?

☐ The biblical text doesn't specify the mark God puts on Cain. In your view, what kind of mark is it?

☐ In chapter 7, Rabbi Eliezer Finkelman offers eight different interpretations of Cain's response to God: *gadol avoni min-so*, "my sin/punishment is too great to bear." Rabbi Finkelman suggests that this multiplicity of interpretations demands that we stay open to understanding Cain in a more nuanced and compassionate way. Do you believe the Torah views Cain compassionately, as a condemnable murderer, or as both?

☐ In your estimation, do God's two sentences for Cain (futile attempts at farming the ground and ceaseless wandering on the earth) fit the crime?

☐ How should we view Cain, and how might we view ourselves reflected in Cain?

7. BEYOND CAIN: AFTERMATH OF THE TRIAL

(chapter 11)

☐ Genesis 4:16 records that Cain left God's presence, then settled in Nod and even founded a city named after his son, Enoch. Why do you think Cain did or was allowed to do these things if God had sentenced him to ceaseless wandering and exile?

☐ The philosopher Leon Kass asserts that the city Cain built in his son's name is a symbol for how civilization has always been founded on violence, fratricide, and the brutality inherent in the quest for power and political order. Do you believe Kass is correct historically, culturally, psychologically? Was civilization the result of human violence and oppression, or a response to it?

☐ The Torah relates that God made Cain *literally* wander, neither fully alive nor fully dead, spared the death penalty but burdened with homelessness of mind and body. Might physical and psychic homelessness offer Cain opportunities for repentance? Ultimately, do you think homelessness was appropriate punishment for Cain?

☐ Was Cain's knowing his wife and having a child a response to his act of destroying life?

☐ As we read in chapter 11, "Eve and Adam go on to bear Seth, and in a sense, Seth redeems Abel from death." Can a person literally make up for lost life with new life? How might we understand this idea of redemption from death figuratively, if not literally?

☐ Genesis 4:25 and later midrashic explanations emphasize that Eve and Adam redeemed themselves from despair, and the world from destruction, by rekindling their love and sexual desire for each other to create Seth. What do you think is the connection between physical intimacy, human survival, hope, and despair?

☐ According to Rabbinic legend, Cain, the murderer of one quarter of the world's population, met his end at the hands of his descendant, Lamech, an example of the Rabbinic idea of *middah k'neged middah*, "measure for measure." Do you believe that we are rewarded and punished (by God, nature, society) in accordance with our behavior, measure for measure? In what ways (if any) do you believe this idea has validity?

☐ In both midrashic dialogues between Cain and Adam, Cain asserts that he successfully repented before God and that repentance made him more human. Does repenting make one more of a human being?

☐ How far can—and does—repentance go in promoting reconciliation in any family, after one of its members has traumatized that family?

☐ Are there acts for which a person can never repent?

☐ Did Cain ever see his parents again? Did he ever meet Seth? What assumptions/beliefs/concerns/hopes underlie your answers to these questions?

☐ The talmudic Rabbis refer to human beings as children of Noah, an oblique way of saying that, like Noah, we have inherited good and evil traits as our timeless human inheritance. What are the best ways for us to balance these traits? Is balancing them the best way to be human, or must we strive to suppress the evil traits and strengthen the good ones?

II. Activities

1. Do a staged or informal reading of one or more of the courtroom transcripts.

Assign each character to a different reader and have all others in your group serve as the jury. Afterward, discuss: Does being one of the characters in our story (God, Sin, Eve, Adam, Cain, Abel, Truth, Lovingkindness) help give you a more empathic understanding of the character? Why or why not? As the jury, what additional questions would you have wanted to ask the witnesses? Has the given testimony influenced your perspective on the matter? Why or why not?

Read aloud two or more scenes in which different Rabbinic commentators offer contradicting testimony. Afterward, discuss: Who do you most agree or disagree with? Why? If you were on the jury, what additional questions would you have wanted to ask the commentators?

Read aloud the scene in which God consults with the jury and the jury asks God to make Cain wear mirrors as his new sign. As the jury, what questions or requests would you have asked of God?

2. Write and/or perform one of the following midrashic "what if?" skits:

- Imagine that Cain and Abel are not brothers, but sisters. Do their interactions change, stay the same, move in different directions? How so?
- God speaks with both brothers after they give God their offerings.
- Eve and Adam show up at the crime scene before the murder and attempt to mediate between the two brothers. How do they intervene, and what happens?
- Eve, Adam, Cain, and Abel speak with their family therapist before Cain and Abel are alone in the field. What happens during the session and afterward?
- As mentioned in the epilogue, we can imagine Moses' brother, Aaron, meeting the brothers in the field and helping them to reconcile before Cain murders Abel. How do *you* imagine Aaron helping to mediate their conflict when he meets them there?
- Cain meets Eve, Adam, and Seth years after the murder and his exile.

3. Create a rap, song, or other poem based on one of these ideas:

- A character in the story talks about him or herself (e.g., Sin talks about why Sin is irresistible)
- A character in the story comments on his or her relationship with another character (e.g., God talks about why God gave Cain this particular sentence)

4. Assign roles and engage in a roundtable discussion of some of the following questions:

- *The political scientist:* "Cain's act of violence repeats itself throughout history on a broader scale. Is the cyclical recurrence of killing members of other groups amenable to a solution, or are human societies 'doomed' to forever play out the hatred of Cain?"
- *The criminologist:* "What truly deters a person from hurting or killing others? Is it the fear of punishment, the appeal to conscience, reverence for God, moral instruction, economic and political empowerment, all of the above, and/or something else?"
- *The feminist activist:* "Read narrowly, Cain and Abel calls for justice between brothers/men, but marginalizes women and the protection of their rights. Does the story of Cain and Abel have clear implications for all human beings, men *and* women?"
- *The feminist scholar of religion:* "Would the Cain and Abel story have turned out differently had the two siblings been sisters? Are men more biologically inclined and/or socialized to violence than women?"
- *The prison reform advocate:* "God was right not to sentence Cain to death. Don't you agree that capital punishment is not only ineffective; it is unjust? Isn't it ultimately a tool for perpetuating class and racial injustice — recidivism too?"
- *The psychologist:* "Might the story have had a happy ending had Cain received emotional support from his family, his society, and/or his God? Is the inclination to extreme violence inherent in human personality, is it cultivated, or both? Can human

beings rein in their violent tendencies with interventions such
as medications or therapy?"

' *The philosopher:* "Are people morally free or is all behavior pre-
determined, making moral freedom an illusion? Is Steinbeck's
claim about *timshol* (you *may* rule over Sin) true?"

' *The moral philosopher:* "Some biblical experts (serving as witnesses
in this book) teach that Cain murdered Abel out of despair over a
lack of justice in his life. Is this a meaningful description of why
people and peoples victimize each other? What can be done to
prevent people from becoming so despairing?"

' *The theologian:* "Like Cain, can any person always receive forgiveness? Are there limits to God's forgiveness? Are there limits to
human forgiveness?"

' *The clergyperson:* "How do we explain the God of Cain and Abel?
Why would God create Sin with the power to seduce people into evil behavior, then warn humans to control our sinful
impulses?"

' *The anthropologist:* "We know that protection of one's in-group
often leads to altruistic evil—that is, doing evil against outsiders in the belief that you are protecting your own group. Can our
story be read as a response to intergroup violence?"

' *The evolutionary biologist:* "Why does Sin crouch at our doors? Is
the human capacity for violence inherited or learned? Is it an
adaptive survival strategy or an evolutionary anomaly?"

' *The lawmaker and the police officer:* "Are any established laws
truly effective in preventing Cain from murdering Abel in every
generation?"

' *The terrorism expert:* "How do we prevent vulnerable young people from, as it were, becoming Cain in mind and deed?"

' *The people all over our planet fighting for justice:* "How do we move
people of influence and power to listen to the crying blood of
Abel and to disable the hatefulness of Cain?"

' *Another role of your choice:* What other questions would you ask?

5. Illustrate or otherwise create one of the following:

- Sin the demon couching or crouching at the door.
- A door that can withstand Sin. How does the door remain open enough to allow movement in and out, while also giving protection from Sin?
- The scene in the field, before, during, and/or after the murder.
- A portrait of the Adamson family.
- Abel's blood crying from the ground.